DIHLm

Celia, Army Nurse and Mother Remembered

A Nurse for the Century

By

Pamela McLaughlin

ISBN: 0-7596-7502-3 (e-book)
ISBN: 0-7596-7503-1 (Paperback)

This book is printed on acid free paper.

Cover photo by: Pam McLaughlin,
Mount Chocorua and Lake Chocorua (1970's).

1stBooks – rev. 01/24/03

DEDICATION

"I will thank you publicly throughout the land.
I will sing your praises among the nations.
Your kindness and love are as vast as the heavens.
Your faithfulness is higher than the skies.
Yes, be exalted, O God, above the heavens.
May your glory shine throughout the earth."

Psalm 57: vs. 9, 10, 11
The Catholic Living Bible

This book is dedicated in loving remembrance to all men and women who courageously and victoriously fought for our nation during World War II.

And it is also dedicated in loving memory to all Hammond Family members of the past, the present, and to all future generations that will come.

2nd Lt.
CELIA HAMMOND McLAUGHLIN
Army Nurse Corps

53rd Station Hospital
European Theater of Operations
European, African, Middle Eastern
Theater Ribbon 1 star
November 6, 1942 - October 31, 1944

ACKNOWLEDGEMENTS

I want to thank personally the many people in my life who helped make this book possible. I cannot name each and every person because there are so many friends, relatives and acquaintances who encouraged me and urged me to keep writing. There were long time friends, people at work, people I met during my daily life or while traveling. To all I say, "Thank You"!

And I received much spiritual encouragement from the spirit of God, through my faith, from attending Mass, from praying the rosary and sometimes from just sitting quietly before the Blessed Sacrament and reflecting.

One Sunday afternoon while sitting in church and reflecting, I received the dedication for this book, grabbed a pen, and wrote it down immediately.

Again, for all the help I received, I say, "Thank You"!

Love and Peace to You Always,

Pam

A NURSE FOR THE CENTURY
"CELIA, ARMY NURSE AND MOTHER REMEMBERED"

THE HAMMOND FAMILY-EARLY YEARS

When I reflect upon this past century, it brings to mind the sacrifice and dedication of my mother, Celia (Hammond) McLaughlin, who served God and our nation under very difficult circumstances during World War II.

My mother, Celia, was born October 18, 1911 in Tamworth, New Hampshire. Tamworth is a tiny village nestled in the White Mountains. The Swift River runs alongside of the village which is located twenty miles south of North Conway.

My grandfather, Edward Silas Hammond, of English descent, was born in Ossipee, New Hampshire on September 16, 1871. He was the only child of Silas and Mahitable, nicknamed Hattie, Hammond. As a young boy of fourteen, after his parents divorced, my grandfather moved to Tamworth with his mother, Hattie. Grandfather was a trapper and farmer by trade and eventually became a train conductor and later on a Tamworth mail carrier during the 1920's.

My grandmother, Mary Ann MacGillivray, was born May 18, 1874 in Pleasant Valley, Antigonish, Nova Scotia. Mary Ann was the daughter of Hugh and Jennie (Smith) MacGillivray. My grandmother had traveled to Boston, Massachusetts seeking work as a housekeeper around 1898 and lived on Otis Place in the city. Mary Ann was a staunch Catholic while my grandfather was a Congregationalist.

They were married at Holy Cross Cathedral in Boston on November 30, 1901. It was the feast day of St. Andrew, patron saint of Scotland. I suspect since Mary Ann was of Scottish heritage that is why she chose that particular day. My grandfather was thirty years old and my grandmother was twenty-seven when they married and then returned to Tamworth and began married life together.

Although it is not known how my grandparents met, I believe they could have met through the Beacon Hill family that my grandmother worked for in Boston. Many wealthy Yankee families had summer homes in the Tamworth-Chocorua area. Perhaps my grandmother spent a summer in the area working at a summer home and met my grandfather in the

1

process. But no one knows for certain how they did meet and were eventually married in Boston.

The next winter their first child, a son, was stillborn and because of the harsh winter months in the White Mountains, the child could not be buried until the ground thawed. He was placed in a small coffin that my grandfather had made and was buried in the spring. The Hammond family was then blessed with many other children, Catherine, Edward, Andrew (Johnnie), Mary, Celia, Charlotte, Charles and Bertha.

Living in the White Mountain area was difficult, at times, because of the hardships of daily life and the various weather conditions. The Hammond family was one of only four Catholic families living in Tamworth at the turn of the 20th century. My grandmother saw that her children were brought up in the Catholic faith. They received the sacraments of Baptism, Holy Communion and Confirmation at Our Lady of Perpetual Help Church located in Chocorua, New Hampshire. Mary Ann attended Mass at this church. Her husband would drive her to church in their horse and buggy and later in his black Ford. He would then wait patiently outside the church until the service ended.

My grandmother was very much afraid of the fierce electrical storms that could suddenly strike at any moment especially during the summer months. Mary Ann would gather her children around the oak dining room table whenever a lightning storm threatened the area. She would light a holy candle, hold hands with the children, and pray.

One day while she and the children were gathered in prayer around the table, a streak of lightning entered an open window in an upstairs bedroom where baby Charlie was sleeping. The lightning streaked down the stairway and into the dining room. It then entered the kitchen, knocking the telephone off the wall and exited out an open window. My grandmother raced upstairs and found baby Charlie sleeping peacefully, but the lightning had etched a burned circle in the wooden floor all around the white iron crib.

My grandmother greatly valued education. Her children attended a one room schoolhouse on Fowler's Mill Road where my grandfather had built his home and owned 300 acres of land. Although, not wealthy, my grandfather was a good provider and a hard worker. When the school closed, the children attended grammar school in Tamworth village.

When my mother, Celia, graduated from grammar school there was no local high school to attend. So for four high school years she received room and board with a well-to-do dentist and his family in Keene, New Hampshire. My mother took care of their three children. She related to me, "I would get up early in the morning and dress the children. We would all attend Mass at the local Catholic church and then walk home and I would get them breakfast. And then I would attend classes at Keene High School, return home, help them with homework and prepare the evening supper. On Friday nights I was given ten cents to attend the local movie house."

The eldest daughter, Catherine, attended Mount St. Joseph Academy in Boston but returned home when the deadly influenza of 1918 struck the area and many people died. The oldest son, Eddie, attended St. Anselm's College in southern New Hampshire.

The White Mountain area, although very beautiful, produced severe living conditions for a young family at the turn of the 20th century. The Hammond family experienced many winter snowstorms and icy weather, but the family learned to ski, ice skate, ice fish and dog sled race. In 1934, Bertha Hammond won the Laconia Dog Sled Championship and a silver trophy. Celia and Charlotte especially loved to ski along the paths and mountains in the area.

Admiral Byrd had trained for his expedition to the North Pole in 1926 on Wonalancet Road and Chinook Trail. Chinook, which means "strong wind" was the name of Admiral Byrd's lead dog and the Chinook Kennels in Wonalancet were named in rememberance of him. The dog died during the expedition.

Springtime brought mud time and black flies. It was also the start of flowering trees and beautiful flowers; yellow forsythia bushes, pale pink peonies, purple lilacs and roses that lingered into summer. The Hammonds liked picnics and fish frys where freshly caught rainbow trout, rolled in cornmeal, was cooked in a pan over an open fire. The family enjoyed swimming in the Swift River beside a large rock which was on their property. It was used for a diving board at the time. They also loved to swim at White Pond, a favorite spot for many residents.

The Hammond children would walk up Fowler's Mill Road to swim in Chocorua Lake with the mountain looming in the background. Legend says that it was on this mountain that Indian Chief Chocorua climbed up to the very top and jumped rather than be captured by white settlers.

It was on Chocorua Lake that Ed "Pa" Hammond would take his children and grandchildren fishing in a canoe for horned pout. And most always on the way back home, Pa would stop to visit his neighbor, George Brown, and offer him some of the catch of the day. Summers could be hot and humid but usually the evenings would bring in cool breezes from the mountains.

one room school house where Hammond children first attended school

Mary Ann Hammond with children
L to R, Mary, baby Celia and Johnnie
Tamworth, New Hampshire
1912.

Hammond Sisters
L to R Mary, Bertha and Celia
summer of 1922

Celia Hammond
Keene High School Graduation
1929

My grandmother, Mary Ann, opened up her home each summer and enjoyed visiting with her relatives; the MacGillivrays from Nova Scotia and the Davises from New Jersey. She loved to make and serve her guests fresh baked blueberry pie after she and the children had picked the berries off the bushes. Another favorite dessert she liked to serve was tender white cake with apple frosting. Mary Ann was a wonderful cook and baker.

As summer ended, the colorful brilliance of red, yellow and orange leaves of fall would cover the White Mountain area. The children would return to school and attendance at country fairs would take place, a little recreation before the winter months set in.

Residents of the area and visitors from all over New England would take advantage of the spectacular foliage season in the White Mountains. Trips across the Kankamangus from Conway to Lincoln to see the "Old Man of the Mountain," a face chiseled high up on a mountain by decades of changing weather conditions, was an attraction. As winter approached, preparation for the season meant canning many vegetables and preserves for the long winter months ahead and the wood pile had to be well stocked.

One of the worst tragedies for Edward and Mary Ann Hammond happened early one morning on November 7, 1929. It was the same year that the stock market crashed sending many people into panic. The incident is best explained by my mother, Celia, who was 18 years old at the time. She wrote a letter to her married sister, Catherine, who was living in Dublin, New Hampshire with her husband Morris. The letter was kept through the years and given to me recently.

* * *

Tamworth, New Hampshire
November - 1929

Dear Catherine,

Early, at 3:30 a.m. on Thursday morning, we had a streak of bad luck. House and barn and everything in it burned flat. Pa's new Ford touring car was in the new shed and it burned also. We only saved the piano and a few duds.

Mary Anne Hammond and husband Ed Hammond
Late 1920's

Ed "Pa" Hammond and son-in law, Chet
Tamworth, New Hampshire
1930's

I was sleeping down at Pilsburys with Ida and Hattie. I lost everything; money and all. Charlotte did too. She lost her cash, $15.00. A little puppy burned up too. Bertha locked all the dogs in the car but this puppy ran back into the house and he howled and burned.

Bertha saved our lives. She woke everybody. We got out the desk with papers etc. and Pa will get $2,000 insurance. He's not so sure about the car though. The silver foxes didn't burn so Pa has to sleep in a tent nearby. You have never seen such a mess. You wouldn't know the place.

Eddie took Bertha over to his house. Herman Edferly took Charlie and Ma. Charlotte and I are staying with Ida and Hattie at Pilsburys. We haven't any clothes or anything. Charlotte and I haven't. Bertha has some and Ma and Charlie have some things.

The two fire engines came up but didn't do any good. We got our two horses from the barn, 10 or 15 tons of hay, 5 barrels of apples, and we got out the potatoes.

I'm going to Boston on Wednesday with Hattie to work. Pa and Ma feel pretty blue. Miss Jones and Miss Rogers gave us lots of food and said we could use the "Key Cottage" but we aren't. Well, I can't think of anything else to say, except we have fared pretty darn tough.

Goodbye,
Celia Hammond

* * *

During this devastating time, my grandfather lived in a tent on his property to protect his silver foxes. His wife and two of their children settled in at an abandoned school house while the other children stayed with neighbors.

A new home was started in the spring of 1930 with the help of good neighbors. My grandfather took his horse and walked up Fowler's Mill Road to where a huge boulder rested by the side of the road. He patiently chiseled out a large piece of the rock and then it was dragged back to his property and became a stepping stone into his home. It had the same magnificent view of Mt. Chocorua and the White Mountain range. A large apple tree was in back of the home and lilac bushes were planted below the front living room windows.

I can recall when I visited my grandfather, during the forties, how the fragrance of lilacs would drift into the rooms. A loving remembrance of my grandmother, Mary Ann, who had passed away at the age of 59.

My cousin Libby recalled an incident to me when she was just a child of five and visited our grandmother, Mary Anne, in Tamworth. Libby was a chubby child and looked forward to having cookies while visiting her grandmother. Her mother, Catherine, suggested she not be given any because of her weight problem. Our grandmother spoke up on her behalf and said, "In this house, Libby, can have cookies." And so ended the matter.

My cousin Libby said to me, "Oh, I loved our grandmother for standing up for me. I always remember she was so warm and friendly." I never met my grandmother because I was born after she died, but wished that I had because of all the wonderful comments I heard about her. A woman of faith, family and courage who persevered in her daily life.

NURSING AND THE WAR YEARS

My mother, Celia, graduated from Hale Hospital nursing school in Haverhill, Massachusetts during February, 1934 and then returned home to her family in Tamworth. On Sunday evening, March 18th, as my grandmother was cooking oatmeal in a double boiler on a black iron wood stove, she had a heart attack and fell to the kitchen floor. Pa and his children gathered around as daughter, Celia, held her mother in her arms and she died. It was a great loss for the Hammond family to lose their mother at this time.

My grandmother was waked at home, as was the custom. In the weekly newspaper, The Carroll County Independent, it was said of Mary Ann (MacGillivray) Hammond, "She was always deeply interested in the welfare of her family and in their education. A sudden heart attack brought to a close her active and worth-while life on March 18th."

During the early 1980's my mother happened to read an article concerning the weather conditions in the White Mountains during 1934. My mother, Celia, was living at the time (1984) with her youngest son, Jimmy, his wife Kathy and their children, Jenny and Tom, when she wrote to me. "Just a note. In re-reading the article, I see it was 50 years ago. I graduated nursing school in February and the next month my mother died. It was a very bitter winter."

It was a winter in which the White Mountains experienced high winds and, in particular, Mt. Washington had the highest winds on earth ever recorded on April 12, 1934. They were clocked at 231 miles per hour. So indeed, it was a very bitter winter, both for the Hammond family and other residents of the White Mountain region during 1934.

Although my grandfather missed his wife, Mary Ann, and the children too, he continued on with his work; gardening and working on his property. Pa liked to sit, in his leisure time, on an old wooden, kitchen chair outside of his home. The radio would be turned on as Pa listened to the Boston Red Sox or the Boston Braves while puffing on a cigarette.

His children, one by one, married or moved to Boston, Massachusetts and New Haven, Connecticut to live or work. Eddie stayed in Tamworth with his wife Lottie. When summer arrived the family would come back to Tamworth with their children to visit.

Many summers I spent with my Aunt Charlotte and her three girls at a small cabin in back of my grandfather's home. The cabin was known as "Tobacco Road". Evenings were spent with my aunt reading to us before we went to bed with a candle on the kitchen table as we did not have electricity. Aunt Charlotte read many books to us and I recall that my favorite was Robin Hood. I remember taking books out of the Tamworth Library as I loved to read and also enjoyed Robinson Crusoe. I liked adventure books as a child.

I can recall the many times Pa would gather all the grandchildren in his black Ford and take us down to Tamworth village for an ice cream cone. Strawberry ice cream was always my favorite. And on the way back home, along what is now known as Heminway State Forrest, Pa would pull his black Ford over to the side of the road where a small stream of water was flowing. We would all get out and watch as he filled a couple of large, clear glass water jugs. The water was the cooking and drinking water for Aunt Charlotte's cabin.

My mother, Celia, recalled later on in life that when the Hammond children were young, her mother would ask her or one of the other children, "Run down to the mailbox and see if my St. Anthony's Messenger is here?" She enjoyed reading the magazine as it helped to nourish her faith. Celia recalled to me how her mother had told her children the story of the six Fatima apparitions that took place in Portugal from May 13, 1917 through October 13, 1917.

The Blessed Mother of God, through the faith of three Portuguese children; Lucia, Jacinta and her brother Francisco, asked the world to amend their lives by doing penance, living their faith, praying the rosary each day, and living good daily lives. The Mother of God foretold the rise and fall of Communism and said much suffering would take place in our world if her words were not heeded.

The Blessed Mother said unless the world repented of sin the next war would begin after a sign appeared. A great light would be seen by many people. On the evening of January 25 and 26, 1938, a great light appeared over Europe and many people reported seeing it. Shortly afterwards, Hitler marched into Austria and World War II began. When one looks back upon the 20th century, it was a century of great suffering, worldwide, for many people.

My mother, Celia, pursued her nursing career working at Massachusetts General Hospital during the 1930's. It was at this time that she met my father, Joseph, but he walked away from his family and responsibilities when I was born February 20, 1941. My mother and I then lived with my Aunt Charlotte at this time with her three children in Oak Square, Brighton (Boston).

December 7, 1941 saw the bombing of Pearl Harbor and the United States became involved in World War II. During 1942, when World War II was in progress and Uncle Sam was calling all patriotic men and women, my mother answered the call to serve the nation. She joined the U.S. Army Nurse Corps on November 6, 1942 and was assigned to Fort Devens, Massachusetts with the rank of 2nd Lieutenant. My mother also signed up for foreign duty.

I believe in time of war, people tend to remember the heroics of men and forget the hardships endured and the heroism of the many women who served in the armed forces. During World War II many United States nurses defended our nation and 16 nurses gave the ultimate sacrifice; their lives for the many freedoms that our nation stands for.

I found it fascinating to look back, from a woman's point of view, to an important but sad piece of history which finally ended with victory and freedom for many nations. Nurses held out hands of compassion instead of weapons and helped to win the war, and nurses were in great demand at this time.

World War II was a war in which the country and its people pulled together in many ways and united for forthcoming victory. The Blessed Mother of God is patroness of the United States. It was a great day of jubilation when Germany surrendered on May 8, 1945 and the Japanese surrendered on August 15, 1945. This particular date is a great feast day in the Catholic Church and is known as "The Assumption of the Blessed Mother." The Blessed Mother interceded for the world, the United States and for the Hammond family with victory. Thank you Mother of God for your love and concern for our nation and for our families.

Throughout World War II, many pieces of my mother's "V-Mail" were collected and saved by family members. They were given to me during the past few years from 1976 through 1998. "V-Mail" which stood for "Victory" was strictly censored during the war and only a few lines could be written on a single piece of paper 8x8 inches in size. It was then photographed and reduced in size to 4x5 inches to save space so that military equipment could be transported where needed.

My mother began sending the "V-Mail" letters to her family members while she was stationed at Lovell General Hospital, Fort Devens, Massachusetts during November, 1942 and continued while she served in North Africa and Italy. The last "V-Mail" letter received was written from Italy and dated, April 13, 1944. The letters were written in a tidy script that is so small it is still hard to read. They tell of my mother's daily life in an army station hospital.

The first letter received was sent to my mother's older sister, Catherine, who was married to Morris Edmundson. Morris had immigrated from Norway. Two of his brothers were fishermen by trade and were lost at sea off the coast of Norway. Uncle Morris was a horticulturist who took care of estates in the Dublin, New Hampshire area.

At this time, I was 21 months old and living with my aunt and uncle who were raising three children: Mary Louise, Libby and a son, Morris. Uncle Morris was loved and known to me as "Big Daddy." He was a great substitute father and Aunt Catherine was a wonderful substitute mother while my mother was away serving her nation.

* * *

November 23, 1942
Lovell General Hospital
Fort Devens, Massachusetts

Dear Catherine,

Just a line. I was down to Ayer last night. One of the girls here is from Manchester (New Hampshire) and has a car. So, I bought the red snowsuit and mittens. I think it will be warm enough and cute on Pammy. It's so hard to get anywhere. I have to rush to work and have been worrying as it's been so cold. Pammy can wear the hat for dress but I'm going to get either red or white double yarn and knit another hood like the tan one for play. Also, I'll send a pair of white mittens. Do you want the hood knit white to match the mittens? I think white would be prettier as too much red is too much.

I'm off duty from 9 p.m. to 1 a.m. and I'm tired as I had to get up at 5:30 a.m. for Mass and could not sleep very well last night. It's pretty cool here this morning. Friday night when we went to sleep, we were awakened at 3:30 a.m. One of the girl's mattresses was smoldering.

The fire engines made such a racket and the sirens were blasting so that I thought it was an air raid alarm and the Japs were here for sure. She dropped a spark off her cigarette before she went to bed and it fell into the bed clothing. We were all up, but she did not get burned. Such excitement!

How's little Morris these days? Write and tell me what color yarn you'd like. Hope you like the snowsuit.

As ever, Celia

* * *

L to R   Celia, Pammy, cousin little Morris
Dublin, New hampshire, February, 1943

Pamela McLaughlin

December 10, 1942
Lovell General Hospital
Fort Devens, Massachusetts

Dear Catherine,

Well, we were told tonight that we were raised to $125.00 per month, plus my 20 percent increase for foreign service which makes it exactly $150.00 per month. You'll get $102.00 every month. I'll get $40.00 and then there is $8.00 per month for insurance deductions. You may not get the $102.00 for a month or so until they get it straightened out.

I don't know and we don't think we'll be here for Christmas because we expect another load of soldiers from Africa (we think). We have suspicions that some of us will go out on that boat. We are busy rushing through passports and everything else.

Now, here's the story. I need some money in a hurry. Do you think you could do this? If there's a loan office somewhere in Keene or Peterborough could you send me $100.00 because I can't leave any debts behind me. If I don't ship out before December 31st, then I can mail it right back to you. But if I ship out in a week or so I can't get my December pay and I can't get my things and it costs a lot to be equipped.

For instance, a year's supply of vitamins alone costs $15.00 or more. Plus I need a year's supply of stockings. Besides when I get to the point of embarkation, we have to pay our hotel bills until the ship pulls out and get reimbursed later. So you can see that I need the money. It makes me mad because later I'll have money on hand but I don't at this time. The Red Cross is giving us some things and they will shop for us, but we have to pay it back, of course.

I filled out a card tonight about who gets my things and where they are to be sent. If I don't come back, everything is yours. We may not get our uniforms until we get to the point of embarkation and then we mail our civilian clothes home. I had to fill out three cards and you'll get one when I arrive wherever we are going. I guess if I get the insurance all straightened out and get the things I need, I'll feel a little more pepped up about going. We were told tonight that if the boat arrives here soon with the patients, the commanding officer will let us have a pass to go home, but nothing is definite. Will write soon.

As ever, Celia

16

* * *

March 18, 1943
Lovell General Hospital
Fort Devens, Massachusetts

Dear Catherine,

Received your letter and, yes, I guess the ten pound iron would be kind of heavy to bring. An old electric iron is okay. I could make plans for the first Saturday in April for you to visit but of course I'm never sure if we'll be here. Also the allotment won't come until sometime in April.

Celia and Pammy-Dublin,
New Hampshire
February, 1943

So happy to hear we have Thomas Patrick, 6 lbs. 9 oz. born March 1st at 3 a.m. Mary had a very easy time. I sent Charles and Mary a card and perhaps will send a gift. His address is 81 Pearl St., New Haven, Conn. Mary and Johnny happened to be there the very day he was born. Leave it to her! She said he was very blond and looked like Charles. I saw Charlotte and the kids on Monday and they are all pretty good except Marcia had a sick spell, vomiting and fever, but no cold.

I hear Pa's okay and he's going home to Tamworth (from Boston). Heard from Lottie and there's still three feet of snow up in Tamworth and drifting. We are having a formal dance here on Friday night. I don't think I'll go. I can't afford to buy an evening frock.

Today has turned out warm and beautiful after a miserable day yesterday. I'll bet little Pammy enjoys this weather. Wasn't that funny about the whale? And yes, I saw those little coats in the newspaper for $8.95.

I'm reading "Look to the Mountain" and I'm enjoying it a lot. My goodness, I'm getting uneasy here. We just sent 8 nurses up to Fort Ethan

Allen on Tuesday. There's an epidemic of some spinal thing. By the way, did you read that book yet, "No Star Is Lost"?

I have only 4 patients with mumps here to care for so I'm having it very easy. I didn't get up most of the morning except to make rounds and go to lunch. I'm trying to muster up enough courage to ask for another 3 days leave.

So long, Celia

A few days before my mother left for foreign service, the nurses she worked with at Ft. Devens gave her a gift and a card. The card had an eagle and a flag imprinted on it. The nurses had penned my mother a note and I might add with a little sense of humor.

"On Otis I, there's a nurse, by gum, goes by the name of Hammie.
In a day or so she's going to go to fight for Uncle Sammie.
Oh, Hammie dear, please listen here to our sad misery,
Why must you go to fight the foe? They be so damned contrary.
If you'll stay here to give us cheer, we'll empty all your trash cans.
If that won't do I'm telling you, we'll even empty bed pans!
But if you must go, you won't be cussed.
All sorts of luck we wish you.
Just want to say, before going away, we all darn sure will miss you!"

Signed by: Cora Lambert
               Angela Schettino
               Marie Messitt
               Mary McCabe
               Marguerite Hogbin
               Mary Lachiatto
               Evelyn Olsen
               Alice Small
               Ruth Small
               Amy Ferguson

After months of waiting, not knowing when she would get the word to ship out, my mother scribbled a hasty written note to her sister-in-law,

Lottie (Gill) Hammond, living in Tamworth. Lottie was married to my mother's older brother Eddie, nicknamed "Old Cap" because he wore an old cap while farming his property.

Uncle Eddie was also a lumber mill operator. Uncle Eddie and Aunt Lottie had a home on Wonalancet Road (Chinook Trail) and were raising four children at the time; Robert, Dorothy, Roy and Stanley, and eventually Patricia was born.

The envelope in which the note was received was postmarked, April 24, 1943, Fitchburg, Massachusetts.

* * *

Saturday, a.m.

CONFIDENTIAL

Dear Lottie,

Just a note. Bye to everyone for awhile. We are all leaving. Next letter you get will be from?

As ever, Celia

* * *

On Easter Sunday, April 25, 1943 my 32 year old mother rode through New York City on a bus filled with other patriotic men and women. Their destination was Fort Dix, New Jersey where a navy ship was waiting to transport the United States troops to North Africa. My mother spent a few weeks in Oran (Algeria) on the coast of the Mediterranean Sea. She then moved on with the 53rd Station Hospital to Bizerte (Tunisia), which is also located on the coast of the Mediterranean Sea, for several more months of nursing wounded and sick soldiers before being transferred to Italy.

The first letter received from North Africa was written to my mother's younger sister, Charlotte (Mullen) who was living in Boston raising three pre-schoolers, Marcia 4, Carol 3, and Mary Jane 2 years old. Aunt Charlotte was also my godmother.

* * *

May 19, 1943 - North Africa
53rd Station Hospital

Dear Charlotte,

Here I am in North Africa in a tent on a dusty rolling hillside. It's very hot during the day and cool in the evening. We sleep six in a tent on cots with netting covering our cots. The first week we slept on the ground. There are lots of vineyards and pretty red poppies here and the damn flies, mosquitoes, lizards, snakes, toads and scorpions are too numerous to mention.

The French people are here and they think we are wonderful. There are Arabs too. I never thought I'd tan but after one week in this sun, I did. The water is full of clorine and tastes terrible. There's so much lime in the water that our hair is turning grey. Our chow is nothing to brag about and I'm not kidding, but we're having fun too.

Lots I'd like to tell you about, but can't. Went to the town of Oran and saw a curious sight. Only wine to drink. Had a glass but what a whallop! Get my address and write. The kids here are already getting mail.

I wonder how Pammy is? Has Marcia joined the army? Tell little Carol to eat all her food. Tell Bertha and Mary to write.

As ever, Celia

* * *

May 30, 1943 - North Africa

Dear Lottie,

About time I wrote to you. I've been sick. I've been in the hospital 3 days, but am much better and will soon be back to camp. I'm not the only one in my camp sick. I'll tell you later. Better not say this to Pa. Did Pa get my letters? I haven't heard from anyone yet. Awfully hot over here.

We walk into a little French town and have a good meal with a French family once in awhile. They roast chicken, serve wine and put on a real banquet. We bring cigarettes and gum. They think our "cigs" are wonderful. They do our laundry and we have to supply the soap. They haven't any. A group of us went to a small French restaurant last week and had a wonderful dinner; steak, pommes des terres (little spuds, the kind we throw away), endives, fresh green almonds and fresh cherries. After a few drinks of their wine my French came back. Maybe you think we didn't have fun! I can't tell you everything I'd like to, but will when I see you.

In fact, everything is filthy here except us and we are none too clean right now. I haven't slept in a bed for so long that when I came to this hospital I couldn't get used to this nice bed because there were no stones in it.

How are the kids and Old Cap? The major just made rounds and said maybe I'd be discharged tomorrow. Guess I'm needed back in camp. I'm very brown now and have lost a lot of weight. Thank God!

The navy men on our boat certainly were wonderful to us. They came up to camp and brought us everything; oranges, apples, grapefruit and water (good). I'll never forget them. They've gone now.

We will not be staying where we are now, of course, but write to me always using this address. I don't know when or where we'll move. It's nice and cool here in the hospital. Heaven, compared to camp and no flies. This used to be a private French hospital. Well Lottie, write.

Love to all, Celia

* * *

June 15, 1943 - North Africa

Dear Catherine,

Well, of all the luck! I landed back in the hospital Sunday but I'm okay today. I woke up Sunday with terrible pains in my chest and back and passed out. And I've pestered the major here plenty because I want to rejoin my unit today. He said I have atypical pneumonia and I say I haven't. Anyhow, I pestered him so much that he said I could go back to my unit this morning. I guess by this time he doesn't really give a damn what I had as I've been such a headache.

Hope you're receiving my letters. I'm writing quite a few. Look in the Saturday Evening Post this July for a group picture of us. It was taken three weeks ago. I don't know if you'll be able to see me. I'm in the center, two or three rows back wearing a white shirt with blue slacks and a wide brimmed hat.

Write and I'll receive it wherever I land. I sent a cable to Pa just wishing him good health and saying I'm okay. I'd sure like to see Pammy now. Are all the allotments coming through?

I'm leaving the hospital, the colonel just said I could go. I'll write again wherever I am. If you write me use the same APO 763.

Love to all, Celia

* * *

Note: Apparently the group picture of the nurses was never published. After checking several months of the Saturday Evening Post, 1943, this picture could not be found.

* * *

June 22, 1943 - North Africa

Dear Catherine,

We are setting up in our new home. Still in tents. We moved quite a distance and you'd die laughing at these slow French trains. We certainly are in God's country here. I miss my swimming. I made the trip fine and I feel good once again. What's little Pammy saying now? I'd just love to look in on her right this minute.

I worked all day yesterday painting the operating room with an engineering outfit who are helping us set up. One is a fellow from Laconia (New Hampshire) and the other is from Barre (Vermont). They made us a vanity table and chair for helping them paint.

I could make such an interesting letter here but you know I'm not allowed to say much. Guess I told you all our money is in French money; francs. Enclosed is 5 francs or 10¢ in U.S. money. I can just send one. Keep it for Pammy for a souvenir. I collected a German and Italian souvenir from the prisoners along the way.

Wish you could look in on us now. The fellows are indeed very busy. I'll be so darn glad to get busy even if it is in a rough spot. The nurses look like little peasant girls here; blue seersucker uniforms and all washing in their helmuts and dirty. My God! The boys killed two little snakes in our tent yesterday. We don't have our floors here, or course. This place is not quite as dusty as our first area. Seems to have a little more grass.

I want to get a few souvenirs to send back to you people the first chance I get. I'll label everything. Boy, do these people soak you; triple the price of everything. Americans have so much money! Hope they bring us mail from town today. I haven't received much from you people yet; one letter from Mary and two from you.

It gets much colder here at night than where we were. We have to get all dressed up at night before we go to bed and the minute the sun comes up it's as hot as Hades. There are more mosquitoes here and we take atabrine tablets every day for malaria. It is a yellow synthetic quinine tablet which doesn't prevent malaria but only lessens the symptoms. It makes some of us awfully sick; vomiting and diarrhea, but we have to take it just the same. It doesn't affect me much.

The French women do our laundry. We have to give them soap and they have no starch. My white shirts are a mess. We are still wearing navy blue. We have a young nurse about 30 to 35 and she was made a Lt. Colonel over all the nurses here in North Africa. She's been here 2 years. She told us we (over here in Africa) are getting all our new olive green uniforms, shoes, shirts, pocketbooks etc. all free and they are nifty looking. Wait until you see them. Maybe some day I'll get a picture to send you. Our blue seersucker duty uniforms will be changed to brown and white stripped seersucker and they are cut very nice.

Love to all, Celia

P.S. You should see our mascot. He is a little French boy whose father and mother were killed in the war. Our boys picked him up after he was found beaten up. We call him Johnny. He wears a sergeant's shirt and pants. You should see him. He's 14 ½ years old. We give him English lessons. He loves it here. I think we are all going to give a little something each month and keep it for him.

* * *

June 23, 1943 - North Africa

Dear Lottie,

I'm fine. We have moved to a new place. Still in tents but here we have an electric light and will have tent floors. There was some excitement here yesterday when we spotted a big snake under one of the girl's cots. I scared him out and killed him but he almost had me running. There was no sleep in this tent last night.

The Mediterranean is beautiful but can't swim out very far because of the strong undertow. One of the girls has a radio and we get American music twice a day. We went shopping and bought tomatoes, lemons, onions and wine from the French people. I'm still getting very tan as the temperature gets up to 125 degrees and is that ever hot! We see movies often. I've seen most of them before but don't mind seeing them again.

All my money has been changed over to francs and I'd give 1,000 francs ($20) for some chocolate bars, a big sundae, a root beer, a toasted hot dog and a cocktail. Instead we'll go to town and get some wine for the beach tonight.

Are Charles and Mary up to Tamworth yet? Remember me to them. We eat in an old villa. My appetite is ravenous since I got out of the hospital. Our chow is much better now. We have to take pills because there is so much malaria in North Africa. Wish you could see the beautiful villas and flowers here. Read this letter to Pa.

Love to all, Celia

* * *

The first letter received from my mother in July from North Africa was sent to her older sister, Mary (Whiting) Floyd. Aunt Mary was widowed at a young age. She lived at a large white home known as "The Pines" in Tamworth on Chinook Trail. Aunt Mary worked as a housekeeper and traveled to visit relatives in New Haven, Connecticut and Boston. I can recall her wearing two piece suits and fancy hats with feathers when she came to visit.

* * *

July 13, 1943 - North Africa

Dear Mary,

Got your letter of June 8th today, so you can see how undependable the mail is. I suppose you're reading the newspapers to beat hell these days. One of the girls got an old G.I. bicycle from some officer. I took it down the road and had some fun with it. We are all set up now and working hard. Lots of malaria. I guess we are made an evacuation unit. Save my letters and should we leave you can follow our course. I don't see why the censor should cut this out.

I heard from Catherine and Pammy says, "Mama is on the other side of the big puddle", and I had to laugh. Catherine says Pammy is very tan. I'll bet Charlotte's kids are getting big.

We saw a movie the other night, "Philadelphia Story." It was very good and I hadn't seen it before. It's old as the hills but we don't mind. I'm all excited today as I just learned some of our plans. Maybe months from now you'll know what I mean. And yes, I think about those pork chops in the blackout in Boston often and have to laugh. Ha! Ha!

Haven't met anyone I know personally except boys who have been to Ft. Devens and some of the officers from Lovell General Hospital. Have to go to chow so will close, and do write. Remember me to all and Johnny too.

Love to all, Celia

Pamela McLaughlin

Aunt Mary (Hammond)
1928

* * *

July 14, 1943 - North Africa

Dear Lottie,

Received your V-mail and package and heard from Catherine and Libby too. It's cooler today and I do appreciate it. Malaria is very popular here right now. Thinking back, we all think we had it with the dysentery awhile back. They find the organism in the blood by a smear. Nothing we can do but take our pills daily.

Catherine tells me Pa is fine. And please don't mention vegetables from your garden or I'll pass out thinking about them. We now only get tomatoes, peppers, onions and cukes and have a salad. No fresh meat yet.

We had a birthday party last night for one of the majors. I had a coke and was it ever good. We have mattresses on our cots now and I can't wake up in the morning for work. Well, I'm going for a spin on the bike. Hope the kids and Eddie are okay.

Love to all, Celia

* * *

July 19, 1943 - North Africa

Dear Mary,

Received your letter yesterday and have gotten them all by now. We are still working and it's still boiling hot here. We had blood smears and they are mostly all positive. Don't know if we had malaria or are coming down with it. The atabrine pills we take usually hide some of the symptoms. Tomorrow night we are having a party. The "53rd" was organized one year ago. Find Life magazine, June 14th issue (I think), and look at the first pages of the book. I wish I could send you a picture of me on the old bicycle here pumping down the dusty road.

We had a nifty baseball game last night. We're on night duty one week at a time. It's dreadful trying to sleep days in the terrific heat. I've had a headache for a week. I sleep in the daytime in wet towels. If it wasn't for the showers, I'd die but I make a dive for the showers and am revived in time before I pass out.

Love to all, Celia

* * *

August 14, 1943 - North Africa

Dear Mary,

Catherine wrote and said little Morris caught a big trout. We have a nice big radio and victrola machine which our officers bought in California before we came. The radio machine isn't so hot but we enjoy playing over and over stale records. "Met Her on Monday" is driving me crazy.

Pammy, cousins Libby and little Morris
Dublin, New Hampshire
summer, 1943

I met a colonel and a major and they invited another girl and myself to dinner at a villa. We had chicken and peppers, tomatoes, apple pie and wine. I never tasted anything so good in my life. The colonel is from Dorchester (Boston) and a West Pointer. Very nice!

Some of our kids are sick already and we are so short-handed. I met a boy from Fort Devens today here in a medical battalian and I had a chat with him. Our enlisted men are from the west and mid-west. We are the only New Englanders in the outfit.

We have a wash room with a big trough where we do our laundry. Also a big long pipe with holes in it and we throw a switch and have a shower. We raised hell about our chow and it's improving. Tonight we had a salad, cukes, tomatoes, onions and peppers and was it ever good.

Keep the letters coming this way and I'll get them somewhere, sometime. I'd like to go to Italy. It's too damn hot for me here.

As ever, Celia

* * *

September 12, 1943 - North Africa

Dear Catherine,

Still living and going strong. The heat is terrific again. I think I'll be really delighted to have the rainy season come. At least it will be cool. Heat always did an awful job on me. Suppose you've been busy. Heard from Mary yesterday and she said Charlotte's kids have the whooping cough.

How did Pammy like the picture of the mountain. Tell her Mama went to work there. I haven't received the package yet. Ask Mary to get my underclothes. Mine are in bad shape and I can't buy any in our officers PX. Also I need a new bathing cap and a suit. I'm off this afternoon and plan to go to the ocean for a swim.

I'll write again, Celia

* * *

September 20, 1943 - North Africa

Dear Mary,

I received the candy and it's in good condition. Maybe you would think they were not good? I have 6 left and it's a race between me and the ants as to who gets them first.

I've been very busy and very tired. I'd sure like to see Pammy now. We are getting ready for the damn rainy season whenever it comes; building ditches, etc. Have you seen Pa? I hear from Lottie often. Just as soon as the sun sets now, it becomes pitch dark here. Thanks for the Bolster bars.

As ever, Celia

* * *

September 22, 1943 - North Africa

Dear Lottie,

Received your letter and glad to hear from you. My God, it's hotter than ever lately. We are almost dead from the heat and working hard too. Sorry to hear about poor Harry Robinson. That's too bad. So nice that Dorothy is going to school now. I would love to see all the kids again but the Lord knows when.

We are going to the ball game tonight and then to the movies. We have a truck that takes us swimming every day if we are off duty. I can't imagine in this heat that it could rain steadily for 3 months. I feel fine except that I have the G.I. diarrhea every so often. Losing weight too, thank God!

You never mention Pa. Did he get my birthday cable? I'll write soon again. I'm on duty.

Love, Celia

* * *

I'd like to take a break with my mother's "V-mail" letters to comment how important the correspondence between service people and their family was during the war. Because of long months of separation of family members it helped the servicemen and women to maintain connections with home, keep their sanity and to keep up morale during very difficult daily living conditions.

* * *

October 3, 1943 - North Africa

Dear Mary,

At present, I've been discharged from the hospital with dysentery again. It's about the 10th time. I'm hoping this cool weather will clear it up and I think it will.

Last Sunday night the rains came. It came down in torrents with thunder and lightning. It blew our tents down and flooded everything. They were operating in water half-way to their knees. We waded in and went back and forth to work wearing our G.I. boots, slacks, raincoats and hoods. However, it stopped raining on Wednesday so I guess the real thing is yet to come.

Today is beautiful and I'm writing on an old box on our stage in a big field in back of the hospital. We had to put up a fence to keep the flocks of goats, cows and steers out of our hospital area.

I keep watching an ant hill here. They are after a dead centipede and in two minutes they will have him carried off. It's part of our savage amusement here; killing centipedes and seeing the ants carry them off. Will write again.

As ever, Celia

* * *

October 4, 1943 - North Africa

Dear Mary,

Received your letter today. Glad to hear you're going back to the Amory place to work. I'd sure like to visit there too. It's dark here now at 6 p.m. and not so very long ago the sun was setting. We set our clocks back one hour about 2 weeks ago. We are about six hours ahead of you in the states.

Glad Pa is okay. They are putting up a tent so we can have indoor movies. Catherine mailed me slacks, the middle of August, which I've been looking for every day but haven't received them yet. We went to the beach yesterday afternoon and I picked up more pretty seashells for my collection.

They moved an old Red Cross worker into our tent tonight. I was so mad that I threw a book across the tent and walked out. Oh boy, if you could hear us beef and gripe. It must sound awfully funny. Someone is continually blowing their top and exploding. Guess they have to in order to survive the army.

Be sure and write and tell me all about Pammy. I keep wondering about Pammy. I know she's okay but I mean how much has she grown? It will sure be a treat to see her again. Ask Pammy where Mama is but don't tease her.

It's all quiet and peaceful here now and we appreciate it.

As ever, Celia

* * *

October 7, 1943 - North Africa

Dear Lottie,

It's pouring rain here and I'm on night duty with my slacks, G.I. Boots and trench coat and mud to my knees. You'd laugh to see me ducking from one tent to another. It's rather dismal here and lousy when the rainy season is on.

How's everyone? Did Pa get my cable for his birthday? We put cement floors in some of the tents and it makes it much nicer but nothing can take away that awful dampness of everything. I suppose the kids are all back and interested in school again. Is Charlotte up to Tamworth?

The cooks are just getting into the mess kitchen and what a racket they make; throwing pans and laughing and talking. Not much like a civilian hospital, especially the way I look this morning.

Things look good, don't you think? We are quiet and peaceful here now. We are all getting so sick of this spot, and I hope we move on soon. We are busy and have added 10 more nurses to our unit temporarily.

Remember me to Pa and read him this letter. How's "Old Cap" doing? I never received any letters from Mrs. Rosebough. Well Lottie, I'll make my rounds and will write again.

As ever, Celia

* * *

October 14, 1943 - North Africa

Dear Lottie,

Nothing much new here except rain, rain and mud. The only pretty things are rainbows, beautiful sunsets and moons between the heavy rains. Glad the kids like school.

We had our first death in the 53rd tonight and we have handled over 3,000 patients which is an excellent record. Keep writing and if we move, I'll receive it somewhere, someday.

How is Pa? Tell him I'm fine. They bought a pig somewhere and we had pork chops and they were delicious. How we devoured them.

I got a letter from Catherine today and she sent me some slacks in August which I haven't received yet. You would laugh to see us wading through this mud with our boots and raincoats. We have a movie theatre (big tent) now with a stage too.

Love, Celia

* * *

Pamela McLaughlin

October 26, 1943 - North Africa

Dear Mary,

I'm sure I answered your last letter too. I'm so glad the underwear and bathing suit are on the way. I received the slacks and socks the other day. I was almost destitute. I hope the bathing suit arrives before we leave. If not, I'll receive it somewhere. Did you visit Catherine? Tell me about Pammy.

I have my bedding roll, barracks bag, etc., all packed and the kids think it's a big joke. Every once in a while someone sticks their head in our tent and asks me, "What time is your train leaving?" I say, "I don't know as I've misplaced my time-table." Ha! Ha!

I don't know where we will be going; Italy, England or India (hope not, too hot). Where is Johnny doughboy? Remember me to him. We are now going to chow and then to see Henry Fonda and Olivia DeHavilland in "The Male Animal".

So long, Celia

* * *

October 26, 1943 - North Africa

Dear Lottie,

Here we are, still here, and I'm all packed to go. All the kids are laughing at me because I am all packed to move on. It's the camp joke. We are all sick of this place. So I finally decided if I packed, we might get orders to move. I think we will before long.

We see some good movies here, old ones, but good. We have a volley ball team but can't play much because of the rain. We saw "Anthony Adverse" the other night and when it came to the part about Africa, we almost split our guts laughing. I'd seen it before in Boston but had forgotten it.

I'll continue now. We are back from chow; roast beef, mashed potatoes, peas and coffee and rolls. Not bad, in fact it was good. Well, have to close up this tent now. It's very cold. Will write again.

Love, Celia

* * *

November 7, 1943 - North Africa

Dear Mary,

Got your letters from Dublin the other day and Catherine's Christmas package. I had to laugh at what Pammy said to you. Sounds like little Morris. I'll bet she's funny. We are all very busy, so I'm writing while on duty.

I got a permanent wave the other day. I went to Ferrysville. It came out pretty good but these French women use the darndest old fashioned apparatus and can't compare with our hairdressers. How's Charlotte? She doesn't write very often. Must be too busy.

We are all busy getting our Christmas cards off. Wait till you see them. Can't expect much from Africa. We see very little sun these days. Mostly foggy weather and pouring rain. We all have colds and coughs. Do you think Pammy is pretty? I couldn't tell by the pictures Catherine sent.

Write again, Celia

* * *

November 8, 1943 - North Africa

Dear Lottie,

Received your letter of September 15th yesterday with Dorothy's first day of school paper. A little late I'd say. Today we have a 40 mile gale, blowing and raining too, and some of our tents are already blown down. We are still in the same place, darn it.

One of our nurses is getting married here tomorrow in our auditorium (big tent). If it were me, I'd wait for the states. Tell Robert I thought his card was so cute and I'll write to him soon.

We are not very busy now after our hard summer and fall. We are having days off now. Glad you had a nice fall; fairs and all. I must be on my way to chow.

Will write again, Celia

* * *

November 8, 1943 - North Africa

Dear Mary,

Thanks for the slip. Very pretty. I expect to get the underwear and bathing suit soon. Gee, we are having a 40 mile gale wind here today and it's raining too. A few of our tents are down. You can imagine what it's like. We all have on our slacks and boots and coats.

Who do you think Pammy looks like? She reminds me of Mary Louise's features but not her hair and eyes. We saw a good movie yesterday, "The Constant Nymph" with Charles Boyer. We liked it a lot. It's not an old picture. You probably saw it yourself.

We are not busy these days. I play cards on the ward with the patients most of the day. We sure have lots of fun with them. We have one Italian boy and they get him so mad. About the only thing he can say in English is "You shut up!" Oh, they are at it again, teasing him. I'll have to go.

As ever, Celia

* * *

November 11, 1943 - North Africa

Dear Lottie,

Got another letter from you the other day dated October 4th and while I have a chance I'll answer it. We have our stove going here in the tent and the patients are all sitting around and talking baseball, reading old magazines and those 25th books.

Not many sick ones now. We are very light and taking it easy. Have a lot of fun here too. I'm more comfortable here, now at night, as we were each able to buy one cotton comforter at the Post-Exchange. Thanks an awful lot for the chocolates and when I get them I'll let you know, but the mail is very slow these days.

I hope we have turkey on Thanksgiving and I think we are going to have it. Have to sign off now as we are going out to drill. The colonel is mad at us and has a schedule all mapped out for us. Well, this is the army!

Love, Celia

* * *

November 12, 1943 - North Africa

Dear Lottie,

Today the sun is out and everyone is washing again as we haven't had a chance to wash in so long. It is awfully cold now in our tents and you should see us going to bed at night in our tents; flannels, stockings and sweaters. We might get stoves in our sleeping tents but I'm not sure.

We saw "Stormy Weather" at the movies. It was an all colored musical and it was very good. We had a wedding here on Sunday. One of our nurses was married. She flew to Algiers on her honeymoon. I didn't envy her any for all the red tape she went through to get married. We are all busy here with our Christmas cards. Wait till you see them. Well, Lottie, will sign off for now. Tell Pa I was asking for him. Will write.

As ever, Celia

* * *

November 13, 1943 - North Africa

Dear Lottie,

Got your V-mail of October 30th. So you can see how much faster it's coming through. Gee, I never have much news from over here as everything is so routine; rain and work! I'd like to see pictures of Charlie's baby. They say he's very cute. Most of all, I'd like a hunk of that venison steak you mentioned about in your letter.

They have started us in on classic drill again out in the rain and muck. I don't mind after we get started. We had fried chicken and apple pie last night and was it ever slick. There's a terrible wind and rain storm here and this old ward tent is flapping and blowing. I expect any minute now to take off, patients and all! We are having quite a few days off now and we aren't very busy. I have off tomorrow. Hope I have something exciting to write about the next time.

Love to all, Celia

37

* * *

November 27, 1943 - North Africa

Dear Mary,

I don't know where the mix-up is but here I am stranded with no stockings. I mean street, not duty, ones. Could you buy me 6 pairs of beige and send them immediately to me? I'll write to Catherine and tell her to send the money to you. Get any nice color but not too dark a shade and not cheap ones. I can't go out anywhere now. I thought they were in the mail and I have been looking for them every day.

I don't think Catherine received all of my letters. I'm glad Pammy is in good health. Isn't she funny! Guess she's coming right along. I'd sure like to see her now. I'm on night duty this week and, oh boy, is it rough and miserable; raining and blowing. I guess you just got back to Dublin in time before that big snow fall. Isn't Johnny doughboy lucky. I didn't expect he'd be around for so long.

As ever, Celia

* * *

November 29, 1943 - North Africa

Dear Mary,

Today I received the bathing suit and underwear. The suit is very pretty and fits very well. Thanks very much. Tonight is my last night on duty and I have 3 hours off now to sleep. Last night I had the most terrible nightmare about Charlotte, Bertha, you, Pa and me. What a fright I got.

Although tonight is my last night on duty, I may ask to stay on as we've had an easy time. I'd sure like to see Pammy this morning. How's Libby doing? Remember me to Carl and Johnny. Is Bill Murray still around? Remember the day I had to phone him in at Park Street Station?

As ever, Celia

* * *

December 5, 1943 - North Africa

Dear Lottie,

Sorry to hear that your mother has been sick. I've just been on a trip with another girl. We flew to Palermo, Sicily and stayed overnight and then the next morning flew on to Naples, over the Isle of Capri and Pompei. Stayed overnight in Naples and flew back to Palermo and stayed overnight, and the next morning we flew to (censored). Had a swell time and saw lots of interesting things which will have to wait until I come home.

No more rainy weather. Have had nice warm sunny weather for the past week and pray it lasts. Went to the show yesterday and saw "Pride of the Yankees". We are busy as the devil here now and no time off as yet. Will write again soon.

As ever, Celia

* * *

December 12, 1943 - North Africa

Dear Lottie,

Just a few lines to thank you and Eddie for the candy which arrived yesterday. It's all gone today and boy were they good. Hope your mother is better by this time.

Did I tell you that our officers shot some buffalo and wild boar and we are now having meat and it's not bad! I wrote to Mary for a bathing suit back in September and got it the other day. But, of course, it's now kind of cold to go swimming. The weather is sunny and nice one day and very cold the next. Tell Pa I'm fine and will write.

As ever, Celia

* * *

December 12, 1943 - North Africa

Dear Mary,

Received your air mail from Dublin (New Hampshire) a few days ago. Eddie and Lottie sent me candy. Did I tell you I flew to Palermo, Sicily, then to Naples and over the Isle of Capri and Pompei? I was gone 4 days and had a very nice time. Saw lots of interesting things and pretty scenery.

Hope Pammy can meet me at the boat but I doubt it though, but she will be able to meet me somewhere when I arrive home. Saw a good show last night, "The Fighting 69th". Very good but an old one. Not so very cold here today but still barelegged with my G.I. boots. Such rainy days. How's Charlotte and the kids? Would like to see all of them and Pammy, of course. Time goes so fast. I'll be here a year before I know it.

As ever, Celia

* * *

December 16, 1943 - North Africa

Dear Mary,

I'm in a writing mood! Maybe it's the wild boar I had for supper tonight. Our officers shot some buffalo and wild boar and we are having meat. It's not bad. I'm beefing tonight, not that I'd be one to criticize the army, but because we have to wear soldier's pants and shirts on duty from now on.

I'm allowed to tell you this now. We had some pretty damn hot air raids here. Night after night we were up and in and out of our fox holes like bunnies. Also have some pretty funny stories connected with them which will have to wait until I see you. One night some bombs were dumped right in the back of our hospital and that wasn't so funny. There were holes in the ground, the size of Eddie's house.

I received little Marcia's letter and picture and thought it was the cutest thing. Our officers are playing ping-pong, the victrola is going mad, everyone is talking a mile a minute and it's time for me to take a shower. I'll write again.

As ever, Celia

* * *

December 18, 1943 - North Africa

Dear Mary,

Got your letter yesterday and I've written a great many letters. Must be the mail is slow since it's near Christmas. Friday is inspection day and we are all waiting on the wards for the C.O. (commanding officer) to make rounds. We have to salute and report to him. All but the ward boys. They all disappear when they see him coming.

We are all working hard and are very tired but not as hard as when I worked at Massachusetts General Hospital. I sent Pammy a doll and layette for Christmas and Catherine said it arrived. Pammy goes up and peeks at the package ten times a day. Write!

As ever, Celia

* * *

December 24, 1943 - North Africa

Dear Mary,

Got your letter and it was nice and newsy. Sorry to hear about Mr. Armstrong. I wrote Leona a little note. We are all decorated now and I'm ready for the turkey most anytime. We had a nice Christmas party last night with a colored orchestra up at the officer's club.

Gee, it was cold this morning. Almost froze getting up but now the sun is out and it is beautiful. The weather and setting are not the least bit like Christmas. Miss our decorations. We have been hitting it up for the holidays and have had more fun. I ran around and squandered some sugar here and there and made fudge for my patients.

Everyone is going to the show tonight to see "Watch on the Rhine" and to sing Christmas carols. What a wild place this is on a holiday. I'll write soon as I have to get up and give my medicines.

Love to all, Celia

* * *

Pamela McLaughlin

Christmas, December 25, 1943
North Africa

ITALIAN TOUR

In January of 1944 my mother was transferred to the fair grounds on the outskirts of Naples, Italy which was the scene of heavy fighting. The U.S. and allied forces had secured Naples on October 1, 1943. My mother recalled, "Snow was on the ground the day I arrived in Naples and Mount Vesuvius was in the process of erupting. The mountain glowed like a red coal".

* * *

January 5, 1944 - Italy

Dear Lottie,

Got your letter written while you were home. Hope your mother is better and that you are now back in New Hampshire from Nova Scotia. I received Robert's letter and it was awfully cute and he is such a nice writer. Tell him to write longer ones and I'd sure like to hear from Roy too. Marcia wrote me the cutest note and enclosed her picture.

I'm glad the holidays are over; too much excitement and parties. We had plenty of turkey. This week we have been up against a terrific wind storm and with the rain, it makes it just ducky. I guess I told you we all wear olive drab pants, shirts and boots all the time except when we go into town.

We had a hailstorm here this afternoon. I'm on night duty again next week but I don't mind it too much.

Love to all, Celia

* * *

Pamela McLaughlin

January 10, 1944 - Italy

Dear Mary,

Thanks for the gifts to Pammy. I received the stockings but have no use for the three pairs of white ones. Glad to hear that little Marcia had her tonsils out at last. I received her letter and pictures and they were so cute.

Probably by the time you receive my letter it will be raining again. Nights are cold and frosty lately but the days are beautiful. Glad to hear you received the candy I sent but am wondering if Pa received his?

Lottie wrote while visiting her mother in Nova Scotia. I'll bet Pammy enjoyed her Christmas this year. Hope I'm with her next year. Tonight I'm going on night duty for two weeks. It's not very busy and easy work right now.

As ever, Celia

* * *

After reading the previous letter, I learned that the reason my mother had no use for the 3 pairs of white stockings was because army nurses wore beige and navy nurses wore white. And, of course, back home in civilian hospitals in Boston, nurses did wear white stockings. Stockings at this time during the war, both at home and for service women and nurses, were difficult to get. While serving in Africa, my mother's Lt. Colonel watched out for her nurses and tried to keep a supply on hand.

* * *

February 2, 1944 - Italy

Dear Lottie,

Received your letter yesterday of January 19th. There isn't much I can say and these letters must sound silly. I have an awful cold and cough and I feel lousy today. Otherwise, I'm perking fine. I bought myself a cameo bracelet the other day but I know I got soaked for it. I don't understand why Pa didn't receive the candy I sent to him. Must have gotten lost somewhere.

44

The weather here has been very cloudy lately but at least it doesn't rain like it did in Africa. Also it seems so nice to see trees; orange and lemon trees. I don't care for the oranges (no taste) but the tangerines and apples are very good.

Till later, Celia

* * *

February 6, 1944 - Italy
Sunday, 3 p.m.

Dear Mary,

At your convenience would you to into Filenes and ask to see the army nurses, summer, beige, fatigue dresses around $14? and also a beige overseas cap like my blue one. They have a maroon piping. Price them and Catherine will send you the money. Get dress size 18 and do try the cap on for size. I haven't a thing for hot weather.

I just came from the 12:45 p.m. Mass and we all took pictures of ourselves on the way back. I was surprised to hear from Catherine that she's been sick. Gee, these letters must be awfully dry. After you write for so long there's nothing left that you can write about. I was disappointed that Pa never received the chocolates as I sent everyone the same.

So long, Celia

* * *

February 9, 1944, Italy

Dear Lottie,

It has been very cold here but we manage to keep fairly comfortable in spite of these smoky stoves. I take it Pa isn't going away this winter. Well, spring will be here soon I hope. I'm getting sick of toting around these heavy boots and pants.

I know these letters must be awfully dry. So much to say, yet, can't say a damn word of interest. It will be nice if Robert won the scholarship.

45

How's Dorothy doing in school? Guess Stanley doesn't remember me very well. Is Roy still going to be a farmer? Did Eddie do much skiing this winter? Catherine said she had been sick with pneumonia. Well Lottie, will close and tell Pa I'll write soon.

As ever, Celia

* * *

February 12, 1944 - Italy

Dear Charlotte,

Here I am back on night duty again in "Little Italy" and it's 2 a.m. I have been working two weeks this time; seven days and seven days with no time off. It was a funny night with thunder and lightning. I bought myself a good looking Italian wrist watch. My other is about to stop.

Thank Bertha for sending Pammy the birthday doll. I dreamed of Bertha last night. I dreamed she was married all this time. I wrote to Pammy and told her I'd sing "Happy Birthday" for her over here in Italy. I hope this is the last birthday I'm away, darn it! I'm afraid she will be all grown up before I get home. Guess I'm impatient. I think when this war is over, I'll settle in the west.

Love, Celia

* * *

My mother told me an interesting story that happened in Italy during 1944 when she was with the 53rd Station Hospital. One day she and three other nurses decided to take a walk but could not venture out very far for safety reasons. The area around the Naples fair grounds had been heavily bombed.

There was a cemetery next to their camp and the nurses decided to walk through it while talking. They saw a large wicker basket and walked up to it to investigate and saw a baby about 14 months old who looked like she was sleeping. She had blond curls and a lovely white dress. They could not imagine who would leave the child in the cemetery knowing the area was under attack. The nurses wondered, as they walked back to camp, if they had seen an angel. It was a mystery!

* * *

February 13, 1944 - Italy
3:00 a.m.

Dear Lottie,

Well, here I am back on nights again for two weeks and are they ever black and cold. I'm sitting here before my desk wrapped up like a rag doll and writing to everyone I know to keep awake. After I finish this letter my head is going on this desk for a snooze, supervisor or no supervisor.

The ward boy is sound asleep. I'm going to get up in a minute and nudge him. He looks too darn comfortable! Besides, he has let the fires get too low. Do you have much snow in Tamworth? I wonder if I'll know what it is when I see it again. No doubt, everything will come back to me soon enough. How is Alice and Chet? Is Betty or Peggy married yet? Do you ever hear from the Fortier boys?

These darn little mice we have in our kitchen are having a fine time. They play all night here and are kind of tame. Guess they know I'm not afraid of them, but the other nurses are scared to death of them.

Tell Robert I hope he masters that violin before I get home and tell Roy to keep hitting those nails with that hammer. Thanks for the two copies of the New Hampshire Troubadour. It almost made me homesick.

Goodnight, Celia

* * *

February 15, 1944 - Italy
11 p.m. and 12:30 a.m.

Dear Mary,

I'll start this letter to you and probably finish it after chow. We eat at 11:30 p.m. and hurry back so the ward boys can go at 12 midnight. It's not especially busy on nights. Army nursing is so different from civilian hospitals.

Well, I'm back from chow. Sauerkraut and sausages which smelled delicious while they kept the cover on. I haven't received the stockings yet but I'm not worried. They will arrive one of these days. I received your funny post card and you've got me because I can't send one back to top it. So Pa didn't go down to Brighton (Boston) this year!

I was just talking to a boy from Beverly and he was so glad to meet someone from Massachusetts and I met a boy from Springfield too. Most of the people in the outfit here are from Ohio and Kentucky. They gang up on us New Englanders. I call them all "damn Rebels" and they call me a "damn Yankee" and we all have lots of fun. How's Bertha?

As ever, Celia

* * *

February 19, 1944 - Italy

Dear Lottie,

I haven't received any letters for almost two weeks now so expect to hit the jack pot soon. Only one more week of night duty and will I be glad. I received a Christmas present from Bertha on Valentine's Day; 3 nice pairs of stockings and a red bathing cap which I appreciated.

The winter is almost over for you people. I hope I won't strike any more hot weather like last summer in Africa. Oh God, that would be terrible. We have a nice new ward room here with showers, wash bowl, ironing boards and an electric washer. We sure do appreciate it after all the damn coal dust.

Another night and all is well but these Arabs are driving me crazy for pills! I'll soon start with the soda bicarb box and they will be very happy. Tell Robert and Roy to write. I would like to hear from them.

As ever, Celia

* * *

February 20, 1944 - Italy

Dear Mary,

Received your "V-mail" of February 1st and when I read it, I don't know why but I just doubled over and laughed all by myself. Say, they should send those two birds over here and up to the front line. Guess there are boys over here who would gladly exchange places with them.

I'm glad to hear Pa is going to Boston for awhile. Got a "V-mail" and a long air mail from Catherine today and could not stop laughing at what Pammy now says. She asked Catherine to write to Mama to buy her a sled next year. Only four more nights of duty left.

As ever, Celia

* * *

March 5, 1944 - Italy

Dear Lottie,

Got your letters and, no, I don't need any soap or toilette articles. I can't think of a thing I need right now. I think they are going to issue us three bottles of Coca-Cola which will be appreciated instead of the vile stuff they hand out here for us to drink.

I'm mailing you a copy of the "Stars and Stripes" which is our daily paper. Eddie and you might enjoy reading it. Well, Lottie, I have a little laundry to do before going to the movies if it doesn't rain too hard.

As ever, Celia

* * *

March 12, 1944 - Italy

Dear Mary,

Got a letter from you and Catherine yesterday telling about Pammy's five day visit with her little cousins in Boston. I would have liked to have peeked in on that birthday party. I'll bet they were cute. They don't look much alike, do they? Did Bertha see Pammy?

I received the three pair of stockings from you and Bertha's stockings and the red bathing cap too. Thanks. I am glad the dress and cap are on the way. The dress may be big but I can always get it fixed although it is expensive. I'll have to pay the price or suffer in the heat in my wool suit in May.

This is my third week in the hospital and they are still doing tests. I'm in another hospital since I last wrote to you and a better one. Don't know when I'll get back to duty next. I'm glad Pa finally got the candy I sent.

Will write, Celia

* * *

March 12, 1944 - Italy

Dear Lottie,

My God, I'm getting bored of being in the hospital. My third week. I'll be so glad when I get out and go back to duty. I now have hepatitis (liver). This is a common disease overseas. So instead of "How's the weather?" It's now "How's your liver?"

It looks lovely out today. I hope the kids bring me mail today, although I heard from Mary and Catherine yesterday. I just finished reading "A Tree Grows in Brooklyn" and thought it was swell. Now, I'm reading "The Family." These are new books. I suppose you don't have much time for reading. Do you Lottie?

If you see a fountain pen for a dollar or so with a stub point, I'd sure like it as I broke mine and have to borrow one.

As ever, Celia

* * *

March 19, 1944 - Italy

Dear Roy,

I was so glad to hear from you, but sorry "Old Cap" got clipped on the truck deal. Do you see much of old George Brown? I expect he is pretty feeble by now. Isn't he? I'm glad to hear you are taking up the violin. Be sure and stick right to it as I'll expect some good music when I come home.

Not much excitement here in the hospital. I take a short walk every day and get some apples and oranges. By the way did you do any skiing this winter? I didn't! I forgot to tell Robert not to take any more tail spins and I'll try and see that I don't.

Write again, Celia

* * *

March 19, 1944 - Italy

Dear Robert,

It was so nice to receive your letter and Roy's letter today. I am in the hospital right now but nothing very serious. Would sure like to be back at work. That picture in the newspaper may have been of us. I don't know. All I know is that we sure landed in Italy.

I went to the show the other night and saw Sonia Henie in "Wintertime." It was very good. That is about the extent of my amusement except when our little Italian boy, with his accordian, comes in to serenade us. He is eight years old and can he make that accordian talk. His eyes are big as saucers and he plays all American songs.

Remember me to all the family and thanks for writing.

Be good, Celia

* * *

51

March 19, 1944 - Italy

Dear Mary,

Received quite a few letters and one from Roy and Robert (young nephews). Roy's letter was so funny that I laughed right out loud. Roy mentioned that Eddie was getting clipped in a truck deal.

Catherine wrote and said that Pammy was so glad to get back to Dublin that she played by herself for 3 or 4 days. Then told Catherine that she screamed when she visited Aunt Charlotte and her cousins because she was tired and wanted to go back home to be with "Big Daddy". Well, I do expect I'll have a time with her when I come home. Don't you think so?

I'm still in the hospital, 4th week now. Wish I was ready for duty. I'm sick of hanging around and censoring mail.

Will write again, Celia

* * *

March 19, 1944 - Italy

Dear Lottie,

I guess I'm getting all your letters okay. I got six today and one from Robert and Roy. Their letters were so funny that I laughed right out loud. I also got the February issue of the "Troubadour" which I sure enjoy. I lay here in bed and daydream and before I know it I'm climbing Chocorua Mountain or basking in the sun on the raft at White Pond.

Oh, by the way, Pa did get the chocolates. My name was on the inside of the package and he did not see it. We are listening to Jack Benny. Good stations here in Italy and not like Africa. Say hello to all.

Love, Celia

* * *

March 21, 1944 - Italy

Dear Lottie,

At last they agree with my own diagnosis. X-ray showed gallstones and I'm happy to know that's all it is. As to my outcome, I don't know

52

yet, but I've had enough attacks to know that it is gallstones and have been out colder than a cucumber. So much for that.

I've been busy this morning censoring mail and reading the February issue of "Esquire" which I sure enjoy next to the "New Hampshire Troubadour."

We are all going to have a nap now so we can stay up a little later and listen to a crazy program "Jerry's Front" which is certainly very silly. I doubt if you get it in the states. Will write.

As ever, Celia

* * *

March 21, 1944- Italy

Dear Mary,

Guess you'll think I'm crazy, writing all these letters but I have so much excess time on my hands here in the hospital and how time does drag. My gall bladder X-rays show stones, which I told them right along, and I knew it was causing all the trouble after the attack I had in North Africa last June. Have to have more X-rays. I'm so delighted the other doctors now agree with me, "Doctor Hammond's diagnosis". Ha! Ha!

It's quite a joke around here now. Only the joke is on them. No fooling though, I'm so glad that they've found out. I'm like a kid with a new toy and it's simple to correct now-a-days. So think nothing of it. Will write and tell you the story as much as I can.

As ever, Celia

* * *

March 27, 1944 - Italy

Dear Lottie,

Such a beautiful day here and we haven't had one for so long. Guess we all have a touch of spring fever! I feel so much better now that nothing is seriously wrong and hope to be out of the hospital soon to either rest camp or back to duty.

Heard from Mary yesterday. Guess Pa and Bertha will be up to Tamworth soon. Wished I was there! Did Roy and Robert get my letters?

Did I tell you we had an air raid recently and were all shaking and not from the cold either. Wished "Old Cap" was here with me. Of course, seriously, I don't. Will write again.

Love to all, Celia

* * *

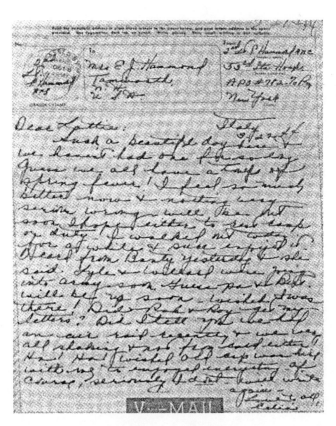

Original "V-Mail" letter
March 27, 1944
Italy

54

March 27, 1944 - Italy

Dear Mary,

Got your V-mail of March 13th yesterday. Use 782 for my APO# now. Today is a very beautiful spring day. Had a little snow the other day. Couldn't see any on the ground here, but could in the distance on the hills and mountains.

Glad to hear they got those Cassanovas into the army at last. I'm still in the hospital. Nothing serious. Maybe I'll go to a rest camp soon and then back to duty. Hope it's not long before we all come home but don't really know.

As ever, Celia

* * *

March 31, 1944 - Italy

Dear Lottie,

Your letter dated the 15th was received today. At this writing I'm still in the hospital but at least they have decided once and for all that I have arthritis of the spine. Had a lot of trouble with pain in the chest and back but feeling lots better now and the worst is over. Nothing to worry about.

One of the girls just went and bought us 2 eggs each at .25¢. We are going to have egg sandwiches tonight. Some treat for us! Now many old hens around here as the Jerries made off with most of them.

So glad to hear that Mrs. Armstrong is going in for war work. Well, going down to look for my mail. Will write again.

As ever, Celia

* * *

55

April 4, 1944 - Italy

Dear Catherine,

Received your letter of March 20th today and was glad because I haven't heard from you in some time. I'm okay these days. Hope Pammy doesn't get all excited soon over the doll because I haven't been out to buy it yet.

Received a package from Lottie yesterday and will be on the lookout for the beige dress and Toll House cookies. Pa must be up in Tamworth by now? Got letters from everyone yesterday.

I sure would like to see Pammy now. I told you I bought her two pair of kid gloves and a pair of brown gloves too. Are you buying anything for Easter? I guess I'll wear my olive drab suit again this Easter.

Will write, Celia

* * *

April 4, 1944 - Italy

Dear Pammy,

How is my little gal today? Did you have a nice trip to Aunt Charlottes? Did Mary Jane, Carol and Marcia play with you? I'll bet you had a nice party. Next year you will be four years old and I hope I'll be home for your birthday. We will have lots of fun.

I saw the Easter Bunny over here. He said that you and Morris were nice so that he was going to bring you Easter baskets. I got your pretty card and put it on my bureau beside your picture. How is Panda, Donald Duck, and all the other dolls? Be a good girl. Happy Easter.

Love, Mama

* * *

Pammy, Dublin, New Hampshire
summer of 1943

April 4, 1944 - Italy

Dear Mary,

So glad Bertha is leaving Boston and going back to Tamworth with Pa. Did she ever receive my letter about the cap and stockings? I feel pretty good now. Guess on Easter Sunday, I'll parade up to the little church in my last year's olive drab suit. Hope next year I can afford a different colored one.

Thank God the weather is nicer around here lately. My God, am I sick of censoring mail.

Will write again, Celia

* * *

Ed "Pa" Hammond with daughter, Bertha
Tamworth, N.H.
May, 1942

* * *

April 4, 1944

Dear Lottie,

I received your letter of March 21st. Not bad time? Yes, I feel better at this writing. Did you like "This is the Army"? I saw it here awhile ago. We liked it in a way but we are bored stiff of war pictures.

The weather here is nice now and next Sunday is Easter so I'll probably be wearing my olive drab suit to Mass. Tell Roy to please get busy on that "gee-tar" as I want to listen to it when I come home.

Love to all, Celia

* * *

April 9, 1944 - Italy
Easter Sunday

Dear Lottie,

In answer to your letter of March 25th. So, Pa finally got tired of Boston and returned to Tamworth. My God, I'm still in the hospital and it sure is a tough job to get out of one. I've developed arthritis in my back and gastritis. Very uncomfortable!

Tell Pa, I'll write soon and that we are not allowed to send any more of those newspapers according to the newest censorship rules. Some of the boys put on a show with bright paper caps and went through the ward and sang Easter songs and funny ones too. Will write again.

As ever, Celia

* * *

Pamela McLaughlin

April 9, 1944 - Italy
Easter Sunday

* * *

April 9, 1944 - Italy

Dear Mary,

I have forgotten whether I answered your letter the other day or not. Goodness, what a grey, dull day it is here. By the way, how was the Easter parade on Commonwealth Avenue (Boston) this morning? Were the hats pretty? I'll bet they were. I will get an armful of those hats when I return to civilization.

I heard from Lottie yesterday and she said she was going to the train to meet Pa and Bertha. Maybe you are up to Tamworth yourself by this time. Did you sell your car or the house yet? Charlotte wrote and told me what a

60

nice time you all had when Catherine and Pammy visited Boston. Guess I've run out of words and space.

Will write soon, Celia

* * *

April 11, 1944 - Italy

Dear Mary,

How goes the battle? The weather sure is nice here today; beautiful and sunny. You will probably be back in Boston when you receive this letter. I've written quite a few times to you folks. I'll bet Pa was so glad to get home. Wasn't he? Did he have a nice winter?

I don't know as of this writing whether we are ever going to get back together or not. I mean to my hospital duty. I guess it will probably be some time for me before I can go back on night duty. Darn it!

As ever, Celia

* * *

At this time Edward "Pa" Hammond was 72 years old and in the winter time he would leave his home in Tamworth and travel to Boston to spend a few weeks with his daughters. And after his wife Mary Ann died in 1934 Pa often traveled to Florida to spend a few weeks in warmer weather.

* * *

April 13, 1944 - Italy

Dear Mary,

Just forget about that APO#382 as it was changed and rechanged. I received the beige cap and dress and they are very nice. I'm still in the hospital. I heard from Catherine yesterday and Pammy requests that I send her gloves and rosary beads.

We buy eggs at $3.00 per dozen and spuds at .45¢ for 2 pounds and make potato salad here on the ward. It's expensive but we all chip in and it's worth it. Lottie sent me a box of chocolates and has mailed me a fountain pen. Must write and thank her.

Till next time, Celia

* * *

April 13, 1944 - Italy

Dear Catherine,

I received the cap and beige dress and like them a lot. Haven't tried them on yet but they look as though they will fit okay. I am happy they are here. I'm still in the hospital and it's a slow process but looking forward to getting out. As long as Pammy expects the things, I'll send them as soon as I get out of the hospital. Tell Pammy I was sorry to hear about Mrs. Dermott (a play doll).

Glad that spring is coming to your part of the country. I know just how you must appreciate it after the long winter. Heard from Charlotte and she's had a hard winter considering everything. Kiss Pammy and Morris for me.

Love, Celia

* * *

Pammy and little Morris
Dublin, New Hampshire
summer, 1943

HAMMOND FAMILY-AFTER THE WAR

The first childhood recollection I have of my mother is meeting her at the train station in New Hampshire. I was almost three and a half years old. I recall Aunt Catherine sat next to Uncle Morris as he drove the car back to our home in Dublin. I sat in the back seat next to my mother who was dressed in her olive green army uniform. And, of course, she seemed to be somewhat of a stranger to me at the time.

My mother's overseas tour of duty in Italy had ended during May of 1944. She returned home permanently from Rhodes General Hospital, Utica, New York that fall to New England and resumed her civilian life on November 1, 1944. After visiting relatives and becoming reunited with one another, my mother and I took the train to New Haven, Connecticut and spent the winter with her sister, Mary.

During the spring of 1945 we arrived back in Tamworth and stayed with my grandfather at his large white home. It was at this time on May 8, 1945 that Germany surrendered and three months later on August 15th so did Japan. World War II was finally over. I do not recall the war years ever being mentioned at this time in our family. If it was, it was not discussed in front of me.

My grandfather gave my mother, Celia, an acre of land just below his property and her brother, Charlie and nephew, Roy, helped her build a tiny two bedroom summer cottage. Years later Roy told me, "Your mother pounded almost every nail into it."

A stone wall ran along an embankment to the property. I remember how my mother and I one morning planted pink hollyhocks along the wall. The cottage had a wonderful view of the White Mountains and Whiteface Mountain could be seen from our living room. It was late summer when the cottage was finally finished. It had no running water; only a hand held water pump and a large brick fireplace to take the chill from the mountain air. We planned to use the cottage to get away from the sweltering hot summers in Boston.

When the summer of 1946 ended, my mother and I relocated to Boston so I could start public school. We lived with my Aunt Charlotte and her

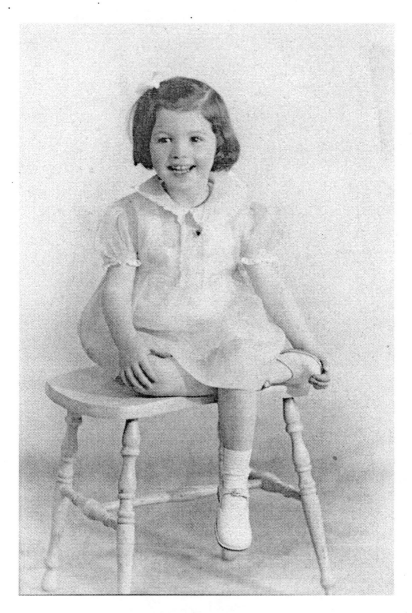

Pammy, 4 years old, 1945

Celia, Pammy and "Margie"
building the cottage
Tamworth, NH.
Summer of 1945

Pammy, 7 years old
St. Anthony's Church-summer of 1948
Allston, Boston, Ma.

cousin Marcia, Pammy, cousin Mary Jane
Summer of 1949

Tamworth, N.H. Summer of 1949
L to R, Marcia 10, Pammy 8, Mary Jane 8 and Ed "Pa" Hammond
standing in back, Aunt Mary

Pammy (going fishing) 8 years old
Summer of 1949-standing in front of the cottage
Tamworth, N.H.

three children; Marcia, Carol and Mary Jane while my mother resumed her nursing career at Massachusetts General Hospital and at the tuberculosis sanitarium on River Street in Mattapan (Boston).

I recall one Saturday morning just before I entered first grade. My mother put her navy blue army nurses cape over one arm. She took my hand and we walked up Royal Street and over a bridge to Linden Street. A seamstress cut a pattern out of the wool material and made a warm coat with shiny brass buttons. I wore the coat and was kept warm and cozy for the next two winters.

It was at this time that my mother met her husband, George McLaughlin, a cab driver. I can remember George coming to visit all of us at 14 Royal Street. He would bring a brown bag of gumdrops for me and my young cousins. My mother and George were married at Our Lady of Perpetual Help Church in Boston, Massachusetts in 1947.

Securing an apartment after World War II was difficult but they found and rented a large apartment at Our Lady of Perpetual Help parish. My mother and step-father then raised five sons; John, George, Michael, Peter and James. It was not an easy marriage for my mother. She had a married life of many hardships and heartaches but she persevered.

I always remember her as being so solid. She was always there taking care of her six children. We were brought up in the Catholic faith. My mother saw that we were baptized, received Holy Communion and were confirmed. She had a lot of patience and never raised her voice. I can recall my mother washing clothes in an old wringer washing machine, that caused buttons to snap and break and ironing for endless hours.

We would put the sign up for "ICE" in the front window of our living room and the ice man would walk up to our third floor apartment. He wore a rubber poncho and carried a large chunk of ice dripping water all along the hallway and into the kitchen. Many mornings one could hear the cries of the rag man as he traveled past our apartment at 1595 Tremont Street. His cries would echo throughout the neighborhood, "Rags, any rags today!", as his horse drawn cart rolled past our home. The rag man bought cotton rags for so much a pound.

I recall my mother cleaning and sponge painting the rooms of her home. After breakfast each morning she would always take a few minutes to sip a cup of coffee, read the daily newspaper, figure out the crossword puzzle for the day and have a cigarette.

My mother was a very good cook; nothing fancy, but a very good basic cook: meat, vegetables and potatoes. Sometimes, when my stepfather was home he would help with the cooking. On Wednesdays, dinner always consisted of delicious spaghetti and meatballs. On Sundays we always had a roast and lots of vegetables and perhaps grapenut pudding for dessert.

Occasionally, after lunch on a Sunday afternoon, my stepfather would walk with me and my three older brothers; John, George and Michael, who were pre-schoolers at this time, to Brigham Circle. We would then take the trolley a short way to Brighton where Nana McLaughlin lived on Hobart Street on the second floor of a brown two family home. Nana and her husband James were originally from Tuam and Connemara, Ireland. Nana was a great lady and I always loved to visit with her. Many other family members would stop by and Nana would always have a large pot cooking on the stove; corned beef and cabbage. The aroma of the traditional Irish fare would drift throughout her home inviting all to dinner.

My mother's daily life was her family. She never drank and very rarely even went out for dinner or saw a movie. She was just too busy taking care of her family and their needs. She was a good mother living in a difficult marriage. My stepfather could have been a good father if his drinking was under control. There was little money but enough to barely make ends meet. Looking back, I believe many women today would have left this situation with their husbands but my mother stayed and endured probably for the sake of her children. And one must remember that this was the 1950's.

I believe what held my mother together was her strong faith. Many mornings she would get up early and attend the 5:30 a.m. Mass and working man's novena dedicated to Our Lady of Perpetual Help. It was held at Mission Church just a few steps from where we lived. My mother had a devotion to the Blessed Mother, Patroness of the United States. She looked forward to attending the church service each morning before her husband left for work.

Our Lady of Perpetual Help Church is a well known healing shrine in Boston. Many healings of body, mind and spirit have taken place since the 1880's and up to this present day.

When I attended third grade at Our Lady of Perpetual Help grammar school, I met my friend, Joan Schubert. Joan is a descendant of the great composer Franz Schubert, who wrote the beautiful hymn, the Ave Maria. Her grandmother, Samantha Sophia Schubert, as a child contacted infantile paralysis (polio) and used crutches and two leg braces as a result of the disease. Samantha's mother had much faith and each Wednesday would bring her daughter to the shrine and attend the novena in honor of Our Lady of Perpetual Help.

One day during the 1880's as they were attending the novena, young Samantha walked over to the shrine. She removed her two leg braces, put down her crutches and walked out of the church with her mother completely healed.

Picture of Our Lady of Perpetual Help
A copy of which was in Celia's Bedroom

Many types of healings took place at the shrine at that time. I can recall as a young child visiting Our Lady of Perpetual Help Church quite often and seeing the many canes and crutches and leg braces left by grateful people healed through the love and mercy of God. I have always believed in healing from an early age.

During the summer of 1952 when my mother was expecting her fourth child, Peter, an epidemic of polio broke out in the Boston area. It was a very hot summer and my three cousins; Marcia, Carol and Mary Jane and myself had gone swimming at a public pool in Brighton. I can vividly recall the next morning; Friday, August 15th. I fell when I tried to get out of bed. I was 11 years old. My mother helped me back to bed and called our family physician, Dr. Doyle. My mother, being a nurse, suspected I had polio. I ached all over like I had the flu. Two days later, on Sunday, an ambulance was called and I was taken to Children's Hospital, Ward 36, in Boston.

By evening, I was paralyzed from the neck down and since I was having trouble breathing I was placed in an iron lung. I remember how noisy it was as it helped me to breathe. I recall a nurse that evening standing in the doorway of my room and telling the nurse who was attending me that a five year old boy had just died.

The Boston area was being hit hard with a polio epidemic. All beaches and pools were closed in the surrounding areas because it was believed that polio virus was transmitted through water. At Children's Hospital all the rooms were filled with polio patients and one iron lung after another lined the hallways on Ward 36.

One month after my hospitalization, my mother gave birth to a son, Peter James. It was a very difficult time for my mother. I recall the many visits that year from my mother and stepfather. And occasionally on Sunday afternoons my parents would walk from our home to visit and bring my four younger brothers.

I remember Christmas that year when Uncle Morris and Aunt Catherine, with whom I had lived as a child while my mother served her nation during World War II, paid a visit to me in the hospital. They brought me a red leather sewing kit and a small Catholic missal from little Morris. My stepfather's sister, Anne Mulry, sent me a gold Elgin watch with a band of hearts which I wore for many years.

And I received a most unusual gift one day just before Christmas (1952) which sits on my bureau to this day. One afternoon a nurse came to my bed. I was sitting up and she handed me a large wrapped box. I excitedly opened it up and there was the most beautiful auburn haired doll that I had ever seen. No card was enclosed with the gift. I wondered who had sent me the doll as I was now 11 years old and had not played with dolls for a very long time.

It was a surprise and mystery until my mother revealed to me, years later, that the doll was sent to me by my father whom I had never met. I named the doll "Molly". A few years ago I did try to contact my father by letter. He never responded so I let the situation go and felt peaceful. But in some ways I felt we had both lost out on our father/daughter relationship by not meeting and knowing one another.

I was confined to Children's Hospital for almost a year having hot-packs and therapy. Polio is a very painful disease in its initial stage. It was six months before I could even stand the weight of a sheet upon my body. A small wire rack was used to keep the sheets up off my legs which were very sensitive. On March 24, 1953 a group of doctors came to my room and I stood up for the first time in seven months. During the next few weeks I learned to walk with a leg brace, back brace and crutches. On May 9th of that year, I was finally discharged from Children's Hospital and returned home to be with my family.

Years later my mother discussed with me what a difficult year, 1952, had been for her. Never did I ever see my mother cry at any time. But she told me that one day during the fall of 1952 when I was hospitalized and after my baby brother had been born, she broke down and was crying in her bedroom.

A picture of Our Lady of Perpetual Help always hung on the wall of her bedroom. My mother said she was overwhelmed with her daily life at that time. As she sat on the side of her bed crying, she suddenly heard a "rustling" sound. She looked up and saw a vision of the Blessed Mother standing in a corner of the bedroom. My mother said Our Lady was dressed in blue and white. She did not say a word but my mother felt immense consolation that everything was going to be okay. The vision lasted just a minute but gave strength and peace to my mother who was going through a stressful time in her life. My mother said she told her sisters of the vision of the Blessed Mother but they found it hard to believe. Personally, I do believe that it did happen, an extraordinary grace for an ordinary down-to-earth woman persevering with her daily life.

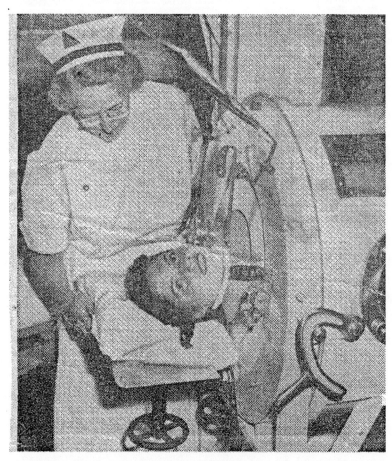

Nurse Ruth Reagan attends Pamela McLaughlin, 11
Iron Lung patient treated at Children's Medical Center
September, 1952

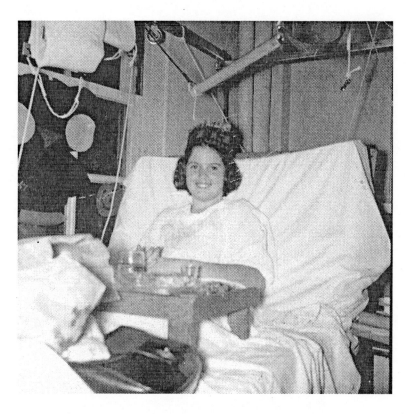

Pam, 11 years old
Children's Hospital-October 31, 1952

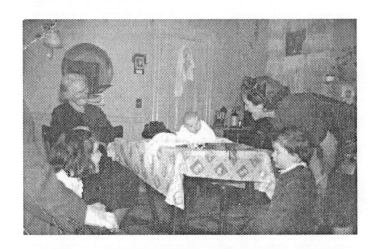

L to R cousin Carol, Nana McLaughlin, baby Peter, Celia
and son, Michael
Peter's Christening, November 23, 1952—Boston Massachusetts

"Molly" Christmas gift—December, 1952

L to R, Margaret Truman, Pam, Ann *Ramsey,* Capt. Thomas Ahroon, U.S. S. Leyte Commander 12th Anniversary of Boston's WAVES—Pam received a check for emergency March of Dimes Drive. August 12, 1954

"Official Photograph U.S. Navy"

Pamela McLaughlin

L. to R George, Celia, Anne Mulry and Nana McLaughlin
1955-Boston

L to R Celia's 5 sons Christmas Eve, 1955
John 8, holding baby Jimmy 1, Peter 3, George 6
standing, Michael 5 years old.

Pamela McLaughlin

During the next two years family living conditions improved. My mother's sister-in-law, Anne Mulry, stepped in and helped my family buy a home in West Roxbury, the lace curtain Irish section of Boston. We moved into the home during December of 1954, the same month my brother, Jimmy, was born. My mother was 43 years old at this time.

My Aunt Anne was always very generous and most especially with family members. Her husband, John Mulry, who owned the Mulry Funeral Home in Dorchester (Boston) had died of a sudden heart attack. Their daughter, Nancy, was only 8 years old at the time and my Aunt Anne then took over the family business.

During spring school vacations I was always invited to come and spend a few days with my Aunt Anne and cousin Nancy at their Dorchester home. When summers arrived, I always spent a week at my Aunt Anne's summer home overlooking the ocean at Fourth Cliff at Scituate.

I can recall the many packages of clothing that would arrive just before school began each year. The clothing was for my brothers and myself. They were purchased at Best & Company, a specialty clothing shop in Brookline. My mother appreciated all the extra help that my Aunt Anne gave to our family.

A week before Christmas a large wicker basket filled with specialty foods, English teas and fancy cookies would arrive at our doorstep from S. & S. Pierce and Company. And always the week after Christmas, Aunt Anne, with her chauffeur driven Caddilac, would arrive at our home laden down with gifts for everyone. She would sit in the kitchen with my mother and stepfather sipping a cup of tea and eating fancy English tea biscuits.

As they talked, my brothers and I would be in the living room looking over our Christmas gifts from Aunt Anne and from our parents. I remember my brothers opening up packages of olive green, plastic army men, some with bayonets in hand. Others were posed in various defense positions. The plastic army men, as I recall, came 100 in a package. For the next year the army men were seen everywhere in our home, behind chairs, on the staircase and squeezed between the pillows of our sofa. One never knew if our home was being protected or under attack. There were battalions of them in all the rooms of our home.

At this time I was attending the Cotting School for the Handicapped located in Boston and was receiving a very good education and was very active with my school life. While in high school I met a wonderful friend, Gail Prince, and her family who lived in Somerville. I have many great memories of my friend and her family through the years.

Throughout the winter seasons during the 1950's, my grandfather, Pa Hammond, would take the train from the Tamworth area to visit his daughters living in Boston. He would spend a month at our home and then move on to visit Aunt Charlotte and Uncle Don and their family. For the last two or three years of his life Pa lived in the Carroll County Home. On January 5, 1963 my grandfather passed away. He was 92 years old when he died and I have such good memories of him that will last forever.

The Carroll County newspaper said of him, "Mr. Hammond knew every nook and cranny of our area, having trapped and hunted over it for the better part of a century." A neighbor said of him, "He knew Mount Chocorua better than I know the inside of my barn."

When my youngest brother, Jimmy, was in second grade, my mother who had been separated from my stepfather for a short while, learned to drive, bought a car and returned to work in the nursing field. For many years she was the evening nurse at The Recouperative Center which was located not far from where our family lived in West Roxbury.

When my stepfather needed to have open heart surgery, my mother took care of him. She brought him home to live until he died several months later during July of 1970. My mother was a wife and nurse to the very end of her difficult marriage.

As the years passed, my brothers and I had left home during the sixties and seventies and made our own lives. My mother moved back to Center Ossipee, New Hampshire for several years after her husband's death. Many times I would visit and bring my daughter, Michelle, who was born August 1, 1967.

My mother always enjoyed these visits and especially with her granddaughter at this time of her life. I can recall how my mother would hand-knit beautiful sweaters with matching hats. She made an especially lovely yellow cable knit sweater and hat that my daughter Michelle wore to first grade. It looked lovely with her long dark hair as she strolled up Spring Street to St. Catherine's school with the brilliance of the autumn leaves guiding her way.

Michelle was always late for school because she would stop and talk to every dog along the way to school. She knew them all by name. Michelle had a great love for animals at an early age. I believe that St. Francis of Assisi, patron saint of animals, must have reached out and touched Michelle with the gift of compassion for animals when she was baptised on September 17, 1967.

One day my phone rang and it was the principal at St. Catherine's school. Sister Mary Ellen said, "Every day I watch Michelle walk up the street towards school. She looks like a Harvard student going to a ten o'clock class but here at St. Catherines we start at eight sharp." I had a talk with my daughter about her tardiness and for a few days she managed to arrive on time but soon reverted to her old ways; talking and patting every dog along the way.

I can recall one day when my daughter Michelle came racing up the front steps to our home. She excitedly told me that a neighbor, Mrs. Casey, was giving kittens away and offered one to her. And that's when Leo, an orange Abyssinian came to stay with us. He was a rather frisky cat and always slept at the bottom of Michelle's bed.

It was in first grade that my daughter met her friend, Maureen. The other classmates nicknamed them the "M and M's" because they were always together. One afternoon I was preparing vegetables for dinner. Michelle and Maureen walked into the kitchen holding a huge bouquet of yellow and red tulips. Freshly picked, I might add, from Mrs. Sasso's garden on Belmont Street. They had picked her garden clean of every tulip planted. After having a talk with them, the first-graders agreed never to do it again.

As the years passed, two more grandchildren were born into Celia's family. Jenny and Tom brought much joy and peace to my mother's life. They made "Nana" smile and laugh over things they did or said while growing up. Grandmothers seem to have a special rapport with their grandchildren and my mother, Celia, loved her grandchildren.

Celia's Grandchildren

Michelle, aged 7 with "Electra"
summer of 1974—
Center Ossipee, N.H.

Jenny 8, Tom 4, 1984

My mother had a much more enjoyable and relaxed life as the years passed. I would visit or my brother John would stop by and take her out for lunch or to the movies. Her son, George, telephoned regularly and would visit once a month as did my other brothers. My mother's faith was always active as she attended Mass or prayed the rosary for everyone in the family. We are a large family and when a crisis arose, my mother would immediately pick up her rosary with the beads of red hearts. She was the prayer warrior in our family, concerned for everyone and praying for all.

A statue of the Blessed Mother was always kept on a table in my mother's bedroom with a crucifix overhead. She had a special Catholic saint that she always prayed to in times of stress; St. Theresa Lisieux known as the "Little Flower" because of her simple ways. St. Theresa has always been quoted as saying that after her death at age 24 in 1897, she would let flow from Heaven a shower of roses; God's graces upon the world. This French saint is a great gift of God to our wounded world.

I recall one such family crisis in which my mother prayed all day for St. Theresa's intercession. My brother Peter had a problem with drugs for many years. One day during the 1980's Peter called my mother in a desperate state and then hung up the phone. My mother prayed all day for St. Theresa's intercession. That evening when she went to bed and pulled down the covers of her bed, she saw fresh rose petals on her sheets. A sign, she believed, that St. Theresa of Lisieux was interceding on her behalf. The family crisis turned around immediately. Prayer is powerful and God listens to and answers petitions.

My mother told me that before she went to sleep at night she always prayed for the souls detained in purgatory. She said that many times she would see white doves floating upwards and wondered if God was releasing souls from purgatory. My mother was a woman of prayer.

When I was growing up at the West Roxbury family home, my mother never discussed her war time experience but later on in years she did talk a little about World War II. I do recall that her 5x7 gold framed army picture sat on a table in our living room. I now wish that I had asked more questions. My mother did share an interesting story with me when I was talking with her on the telephone one day. I asked my mother to write it down and mail it to me which she did.

* * *

Celia and son, John-Christmas 1986

March 1, 1978
Center Ossipee, New Hampshire

THE SMILE IN THE LEMON GROVE

During World War II, I was an army nurse. My unit was set up on the fair grounds outside of Naples, Italy. One Sunday, after attending Mass in a bombed out chapel, I was walking back to quarters through a lemon grove. I noticed a line of enlisted men who were ascending steps to a raised platform.

Curious as to who the celebrity might be, I also stepped in line and climbed up to the stage. I saw a man signing autographs. Even though there were men ahead of me, he turned his head and beckoned me to come forward. As I approached him, I was greeted by one of the biggest and happiest smiles that I have ever received.

He then shook my hand and wrote "Joe E. Brown" on the inside cover of my prayer missal. I returned to my outfit elated and greatly uplifted in spirit. Today, when I reminisce and think back to that day and look at his signature, I just have to smile back in return at his famous smile that meant so much to me, that day a long time ago.

* * *

My mother always kept a nurse's heart of compassion with patients and family members through the years. When family members were sick or dying, she made herself available. Looking back, it was a stressful time for me in 1973 when I was diagnosed with uterine cancer that year. My daughter, Michelle, was only six years old and had just started first grade at St. Catherine of Genoa School. As a single mother, I was her sole support and working in Boston as a part-time secretary for the Boston Stock Exchange.

In September of 1973, my doctor told me I needed to have a hysterectomy. But I developed pneumonia and had to wait until my lungs cleared before having the operation. My doctor advised me to leave work and rest. But how can you when you are supporting your household? It took until Thanksgiving for my lungs to finally clear, much longer than expected. With Christmas around the corner I told my doctor I would have the operation after Christmas. I wanted to make certain Michelle had a wonderful Christmas, not really knowing what was going to happen. Cancer can be a frightening illness. One never knows what will be faced during treatment. But with faith in God the road is easier, no matter what the outcome.

I remember telling Michelle that year that she could ask Santa Claus for one present only. And she did, although now, I cannot remember what gift she requested. On Christmas morning I can still hear her walking up the hallway to the living room and hearing her gasp at the many gifts that were under the Christmas tree. I wanted it to be a special Christmas for her, not knowing what might happen to me. She ran down the hall to my bedroom and said, "Mama get up and see all the presents that Santa left for me!"

Finally, the day after Christmas (1973) I went to the hospital. I had the operation and recovered quite well afterwards. My doctor felt that since I had polio and used Canadian crutches recovery might take longer than usual. But, thank God, it didn't and I was back to work in five weeks. And of course, my mother being the nurse that she was, came and stayed with me and Michelle for a week until I felt better. And I thank Jesus for His love and mercy to me and my daughter that I didn't need any further treatments.

Ever since my bout with cancer, I have always tried to help the sick, the disabled and, most especially, people with cancer through prayer or encouragement. I have shared God's goodness to me and my family at my prayer group for many years or whenever I unexpectedly meet someone during my daily life. Today, people need to know that the presence of God is alive through our faith in a variety of ways. He cares for us more than we, as His people, can ever care for ourselves.

I always carry blessed oil with me from St. Joseph's Oratory in Montreal, Canada. Blessed Brother Andre, a great healer of God, lived and worked at St. Joseph's Oratory for decades. I have visited this shrine many times and have received so many graces.

Just recently a long-time friend of mine, Joanie Gendrolis, telephoned to say she needed to have further biopsy treatment done, as the first biopsy looked cancerous. I sent her some blessed oil from the Oratory. I told my friend I would pray for her as I was just leaving to visit Montreal and Quebec on a four day pilgrimage

When I returned from the pilgrimage, Joanie asked if I would pick her up at the Boston hospital the day the biopsy tests were scheduled. That day when the tests were completed, I drove to the hospital and picked up my friend of 38 years. Joanie commented to me on the drive back to her home, "The doctor said it didn't look bad." But then Joanie added, "Maybe it's not good either." I said, "Let's just wait and see. Bless yourself with the oil."

A few days later on Thursday, August 9, (2001) Joanie called and said happily, "I just received a call from my doctor's office and there's no cancer." We both breathed a sigh of relief. I remarked to my friend, "That's great news. Do you realize that today is the birthday of Blessed Brother Andre. He must have interceded for you to Jesus."

Pamela McLaughlin

THE WEDDING

Another wonderful, grace filled and blessed shrine is St. Anne-de-Beaupre located in Quebec, Canada. Many healings of body, mind and spirit have taken place at this shrine dedicated to Saint Anne, mother of the Blessed Mother and grandmother of Jesus.

Recently, I made a pilgrimage to St. Anne's shrine to pray for a special intention for my daughter, Michelle and her friend, Frank Escobedo, a hard working engineer from Cheyenne, Wyoming. I prayed that after knowing one another for quite some time they would get married. Within a short time of returning home from the pilgrimage I could see signs of marriage in the making.

One afternoon I visited Michelle and Frank to have supper with them. Frank was busy painting a wooden board under a canopy that he had set up under a tree. Michelle came out the door holding a tray of condiments for our barbecue. I had just watched the news on television. The famous singer, Barbara Streisand, had just married her long-time friend under a canopy in California. I just could not resist as I said to my daughter, "Michelle, Barbara Streisand just got married under a canopy. Are you and Frank planning to get married?" She smiled and said, "Ma, you had better ask Frank."

A few months later Frank gave Michelle a lovely diamond ring. They announced the good news and she displayed her ring to the family during Christmas Day dinner (1999) at cousin Patty's home. Marriage plans were then made for June 10, 2000 at St. Catherine of Genoa Church. It was such a beautiful wedding day. All the months of planning came together on this Saturday at 12 noon. Many guests from all over the United States came for the wedding. Frank's mother, Josephine, his sisters, brothers and relatives had flown in from Wyoming for the ceremonies.

As I sat in a pew and waited at St. Catherine's church for the music to begin, I thought of the many parish activities I had been involved in while a parishioner at this church. For twenty years I was an active member of St. Catherine Women's Guild. I enjoyed my church work sponsoring communion suppers and helping at many annual bazaars and raising much money with these endeavors. Many friendships were formed at this time.

My close friend, Donna Fantasia, was also very active with parish activities when our girls were attending school here and we lived in the parish. Donna and I both smile when we reminisce about the time she made 200 meatballs for a parish function.

I recall the time I ran my first communion supper on Monday evening during May of 1977. I had received a response that 56 parishioners were planning to attend, but after Mass that evening 117 people showed up at the hall for supper. I had prepared much of the food and knew there was not enough to feed 61 extra people that evening.

Since I was the chairlady of this event, I stood in the kitchen extremely tense as I said to several guild members who were helping, "Put the food out and let them come and eat." Immediately, 117 hungry people lined up inside of St. Catherine's hall and were fed, each and everyone. One of the parishioners, Betty, came over to me and said, "Pam get something to eat!" I walked over to the buffet table. There was enough for one more plate and not one person asked for seconds.

As I glanced around the hall, with fresh flowers on each oblong table, I saw many friends chatting away and enjoying themselves including many past presidents of the women's guild and most notably, Mary, a member of many years.

There was no question in my mind that God supplied our needs twice that evening. By feeding us with His Body and Blood during Mass and nourishing our souls. Then once again, by feeding our bodily needs and spirits at St. Catherine's hall. A wonderful time was had by all. Not many parishioners attending the communion supper knew that a multiplication of food had taken place that evening. But God knew and I knew exactly what had taken place. He takes care of us more than we can ever provide for ourselves.

My mind drifted back inside of St. Catherine's Church as I patiently waited for my daughter to walk down the aisle. The music in the choir loft began and I reflected on the many years I had climbed up the stairs with my crutches and sang in the choir. Sister Eleanor was a wonderfully gifted choir director who had studied music in France. I have always loved music. To me, singing soothes the soul and heals the spirit. Sister Eleanor and her prayerful friend, Sister Mary, both now retired were two of the most dedicated and hospitable parish nuns I have ever had the pleasure of knowing.

And speaking of "dedication and hospitality" who can ever forget the generosity of the "Little Sisters of the Poor" whose motherhouse is located in France. They work exclusively with the elderly by feeding, housing and taking care of all their needs. I personally know many of the sisters from visiting their home which is located a short distance from where I live. My hometown of Somerville is so very blessed to have these nuns in our community, throughout the United States and all over the world. They are a wonderful, devoted order of nuns that God has blessed and given to us, His people.

As I sat in the pew, I glanced at my watch. It was 12:15 p.m. and Frank was late for his wedding. Usually, it's my daughter who is always late. And I thought, "Michelle will never let him forget it," and smiled inwardly.

And reflecting back to my daughter's school years at St. Catherine's school, I thought about when she was chosen to crown the Blessed Mother during May one year just before eighth grade graduation. Michelle was wearing a long white gown embossed with white roses and was wearing her first pair of high heels on the altar for all to see. I watched as Michelle climbed up a steep ladder with a fresh wreath of flowers to crown Our Lady.

My daughter placed the crown on Mary's head and just at that moment, Father John Carr, the pastor, led the congregation in song, singing verse after verse of "Immaculate Mary, your praises we sing!" Michelle looked rather tense. She told me afterwards that she felt like she was going to fall off the ladder. If she was looking for any sympathy from me, she didn't get it as I remarked, "Well, that's what you get for insisting on buying those spike heels."

I thought of the many Midnight Eve masses Michelle and I attended at St. Catherine's Church. She was just eight years old when we first began attending Midnight Mass. After Mass we would walk up Highland Avenue to our apartment building around 1:30 a.m. on Christmas morning.

I recall one Christmas as my daughter and I were walking back home early one morning, Father Carr, driving his car, stopped and gave us a ride to the entrance of our building. He had several loaves of Irish bread next to him in the front seat. As Michelle and I got out of the car and as I was adjusting my Canadian crutches, Father Carr said, "Merry Christmas to the

Pam and daughter, Michelle
friend's 90th birthday party, June, 1994

front, Michelle and Maureen (best friends)
St. Catherine's Drill Team-April, 1980

two of you!" He handed us a large loaf of Irish bread which I knew was made by the Little Sisters of the Poor. The bread is a specialty at their home and they make it at certain times of the year. Christmas is one of those special occasions.

My thoughts were suddenly interrupted as the sounds of the traditional wedding march with a trumpet accompaniment, could now be heard throughout St. Catherine's Church. Frank was now standing near the altar waiting with his brother, Mark, who would be the best man. Maureen, my daughter's childhood friend since first grade, was waiting in attendance to be matron of honor with her two children, Shannon and Caitlyn, who were the flower girls along with other wedding party members, Jean, Laura, Terry, Seth and friends.

I saw my daughter with her father by her side walking down the aisle. Michelle looked radiant. I was happy to see she had chosen the lace appliqué dress with a 20 foot train that I particularly liked. My daughter had picked out three dresses but had kept secret until today what dress she would actually wear for her wedding. Around her neck Michelle was wearing a lovely strand of white pearls. My mother Celia was given a three strand set of pearls by her sister-in law, Anne Mulry when she was married. My mother gave the pearls to me and I had a jeweler separate them into three strings of pearls. One I gave to Michelle, another to my niece, Jenny and the last string I kept for myself. Two lovely wicker baskets of blue hydrangeas could be seen in front of the altar.

Friends said to me before the wedding, "Pam, are you going to cry?" I replied, "Of course not. I am going to feel joy, absolute joy!" And it was a most joyous occasion for me as Frank Escobedo and Michelle Farino were united in a covenant and sacrament of marriage. I listened as they recited their vows to one another of love, in sickness and in health, till death do us part. Their vows were very meaningful as they knelt at the altar of God and pledged their love for one another with gold rings of fidelity.

It was a happy occasion, for me as a parent and mother, when my daughter and son-in-law, as man and wife, turned around to leave the altar and walked back up the aisle to the applause of many friends and relatives. And I knew in my heart that the pilgrimage I had made to St. Anne-de-Beaupre was blessed and that St. Anne had interceded for the well being of my family. The saints are always there to help us with the joys and struggles of our daily lives.

As I left St. Catherine's church that day for the ride to the reception I thought of the many blessings that have come from making pilgrimages through the years. I first began traveling to Europe in 1964. I have always loved to travel and meet new people and to see the world. Even when I was young, I began traveling by train with my mother and loved it. Later on in life, I planned trips by myself to Canada, France, Ireland, Italy, Fatima, Portugal, Russia, Spain, Israel and Mexico and other countries have always fascinated me through the years.

My Aunt Catherine had a picture of Mont Saint Michael located in France hanging on her living room wall. When I was a child I was always drawn to this picture. In 1964, I saw an ad in the travel section for a 21 day trip to Europe. A picture of Mont Saint Michael was in the ad and I knew I had to sign up for the trip.

I told my mother of my upcoming adventure. I was 23 years old at the time and she remarked, "Well, do you think it's safe to go?" Considering her World War II adventures she surprised me with that comment. I answered, "Ma, of course I'm going." I went and had a great time visiting England, France, Switzerland and many other countries. I was with a bus group of 35 people. We had a wonderful three weeks traveling abroad. After that first European experience, whenever, I had the opportunity to travel, I packed my bag and traveled. Traveling is a great education.

As I was being driven to the Steven's Estate where Michelle and Frank were going to have their reception, I reflected back to a strong guiding spiritual father in my life. For many years I have prayed to Padre Pio for his love and guidance in many daily situations. I can recall during May of 1978 my daughter Michelle and I traveled to Switzerland for a week. We were in the process of trying to find new housing and not knowing where we would relocate.

This was a particularly difficult time in my life, knowing that the house where we were living had been sold and I had to find suitable housing for the two of us. I had booked the trip to Switzerland three months earlier and tried to back out of the trip but was not able to. So we packed our bags and flew from Boston to Geneva during the wonderful month of May. As we were descending into Geneva, I recall the glory of God was so evident in the cloud formation. The clouds were spectacular; a vision of God's glory.

Michelle and I arrived in Geneva only to be told the hotel our group was staying at was overbooked. So instead our group was given accommodations at new condominiums built on the top of a mountain. My daughter and I were given a large two bedroom apartment. When we stepped outside of the doorway each morning to take a bus down the steep mountain, the Matterhorn in all its splendor could be seen. So close, we could almost reach out and touch it.

Each day, my eleven year old daughter Michelle and I would take the bus to a different city and town and explore its many treasures. We both loved Geneva and twice traveled to the picturesque city. We walked along Lake Geneva with the French Alps as a background. It was here on Mother's Day that Michelle and I had dinner on the second floor of a restaurant overlooking Lake Geneva and the French Alps. I recall we both had minute steak, French fries and salad. Just as dinner ended, the waiter came over, handed me a long stemmed red rose and said with a smile, "Happy Mother's Day!" And it was a happy, peacefilled Mother's Day.

After dinner my daughter and I took a walk along the boardwalk and then took a trolley a short way to the Castle of Chillon. Many tourists were visiting that day and I remember looking at the steep cobblestone entry way into the castle. For safety reasons, I decided it was best to wait until Michelle toured the castle. She ran into the castle and disappeared for one half hour or so. When she arrived back she exclaimed, "It was great!" And we continued on our way.

Another day when we visited Geneva, we toured the city and visited a gift shop. Michelle bought a small clock and I purchased a Hummel music box with two children on top; a girl reading a book and a boy playing an accordion. Mementoes for the future. I recall that day we had lunch at an Italian restaurant and then Michelle and I walked towards the train station for the trip back to our condominium.

Along the way we passed a church, the Notre Dame, I believe. It looked closed as the bushes in front needed care. I said to my daughter, "Go up and see if it is open so we can pay a visit!" I watched as Michelle ran up the steps and tried the door. It opened and one could see the light inside. We walked in and no one seemed to be there as we walked down the left aisle to the side altar.

Immediately, I saw a lovely statue of the Blessed Mother beautifully adorned. Of course it was the month of May and as Catholics we honor the Mother of God. Someone had taken glossy pictures of Our Lady of Fatima Statue and had left them in front of the statue. I took one for myself and one for my daughter. I noticed that a large floral bouquet of Birds of Paradise had been left beside the statue in honor of the Blessed Mother. As I stood before the statue I said a prayer asking for help and guidance with my daily life. A prayer from the heart.

As I finished my prayer, I noticed someone else was present. A Capuchin monk, short in stature, with his head bowed slightly and the brown hood of his cassock covering his head. He walked slowly back and forth and I was struck by his presence and really didn't know why.

My daughter and I flew back to Boston, found new housing, and went about daily life. It was during the early eighties that I joined the Padre Pio Prayer Group in Cambridge, Massachusetts. It was a friend, Evelyn Crotty, mother of eight children, who introduced me to Padre Pio. One of the blessings I have received in life is to have the love and guidance of a spiritual father, Padre Pio of San Giovanni, Italy.   He is the only stigmatized Catholic priest. He had the five bleeding wounds of Christ for 50 years. Padre Pio died on September 23, 1968 and he is a great spiritual father to many people. I visited San Giovanni in 1998 and prayed at the tomb of Padre Pio. It was raining that day. Many people were praying at the tomb. Padre Pio had many spiritual gifts; gifts of healing, bilocation; he could be in two places at the same time. He was a great confessor and could look into a person's soul as they went to confession with him. Many people, including myself, have known his presence through the fragrance of perfume; sometimes lilacs, incense, roses or a multi-fragrance of flowers.

I was baptized on September 20, 1941 at Our Lady of Lourdes Church in Boston and it happened to be the 23rd anniversary of the day that Padre Pio received the stigmata, the bleeding wounds of Christ. Padre Pio took many spiritual children under his wings, like an angel of God, and prayed for them. And I do believe especially during World War II, that he prayed for many abandoned children and children who would need spiritual guidance throughout their lives.

Although my mother did not visit Padre Pio when she was a nurse in Italy during World War II, many servicemen did get the opportunity to do so and were blessed by being in his presence and attending Mass. It was said there was a reverence and holiness in the way Padre Pio celebrated the Eucharist with such love and devotion to Christ. Padre Pio touched many souls. I cannot help but wonder if on that day in May of 1978 in Geneva, Switzerland at Notre Dame Church, if that was Padre Pio walking slowly back and forth with our Lady looking down upon us all. Even after Padre Pio's death in 1968, people have reported seeing him and receiving his help. Padre Pio, a great saint, is due to be canonized very soon.

Frank and Michelle—Wedding Day
with family pets
Cheyenne, Kyja, Pooh-Bear and Pudgeè
June 10, 2000

Wedding Day-June 10, 2000
Michelle and Frank with family at reception

Well, I've certainly done much reflecting while on the way to my daughter's wedding reception. I could see Michelle and Frank chatting away in the Rolls Royce in front of me.

It was mid-afternoon by the time the wedding party, friends and relatives arrived at the Steven's Estate where Frank and Michelle planned to have their reception. A large tent was out on the lawn. It was ninety degrees but still comfortable with a light breeze as the 200 guests sat down to dinner, I noticed that Michelle and Frank went to such lengths to make sure their guests would enjoy their wedding.

The best man gave the toast and ended by saying, "May your love always remain traditional!" And what better way for a married couple than to remain solid and traditional. Lovely flowers and ice sculptures could be

99

seen inside the estate and under the tent. An orchid was placed on each dinner plate. My brother, John, a chef and baker remarked, "Dinner was superb!" It consisted of filet mignon with huge stuffed shrimp or chicken piccata which I chose. My friend, Joanie Gendrolis, who sat next to me, offered me one of her shrimp. It was delicious. My brother, Jimmy and his wife, Kathy and daughter, Jenny had come from Florida and were enjoying the festivities. Karen, a family friend, had also arrived from Florida.

For all the invited guests a large punch bowl sat on each round table with pink and blue colored marbles on the bottom. A colorful Siamese fighting fish was swimming inside with candles floating on top. On the side of the tent was a large pen with flowers adorning the edge of it. Frank and Michelle's four Chinese Shar-Peis were watching the events unfold. Pooh-bear was wearing a tux and his top hat was hanging by the side of the pen. Michelle who works in the veterinary field could not leave her faithful pets at home, even on her wedding day. As "family members" they had to be invited to the reception. Many veterinary people, college friends and work people attended.

It was wonderful seeing all our family and friends having such a good time. My cousin, Libby, had come from California to share in this special day. Libby is now a retired teacher. My cousin Marcia and her husband Lee arrived from New York. Their son, Mark, was not able to attend as he has a back injury. Marcia misses her family living so far from Boston. She keeps in touch with everyone by sending cards and when Christmas arrives, so does a package from Marcia and Lee. And I can always expect that in the package will be an item to remember when we were children growing up together, an antique ornament or a special box of candy. Memories of the past.

I saw my cousin Carol and her husband, Paul Amirault dancing away on the wooden floor. Carol and Paul have been an anchor in the Hammond family through the years at Thanksgiving, Christmas, Easter, Memorial Day, summer barbecues or special family get togethers. Either they or their children will host the affair and the family will come and enjoy the day. I have always loved the family weddings, showers and christenings and other get togethers we have celebrated during the past years. It's a time for our family to reconnect, reunite and continue on with the

Hammond Family generations. It's important not to ever forget our roots; not only our Christian roots but also our family roots.

As I glanced out to the lawn, I could see cousin Michael and his wife Gloria with their two boys, Michael and David. Gloria was expecting another child to add to her family and to the Hammond generations. The two boys were running and jumping and having a wonderful time. Gloria looked a little tired as she was due most any day now. (Six days after the wedding, Michael and Gloria became the proud parents of baby Douglas).

Our young cousin Shannon from Washington, D.C. could be seen chatting with family members. While on the dance floor, I saw Tom Hammond and his wife, Ellen from Omaha, Nebraska. Tom was the baby boy that my mother mentioned in her letter of March 18, 1943 when she

cousin Carol and Pam-Thanksgiving Day, 1997

Pamela McLaughlin

Thanksgiving dinner, November, 1999
L to R, Michelle, cousin Paul Amirault and Frank Escobedo

Hammond descendants (cousins) July, 2000-Birthday Party
Front, L to R, Michelle, Susan, Laura
Back row, L to R, Patty, Chris, Terry, Charlotte

Catholic Daughters of America visiting
The Basilica of the National Shrine of the Assumption of the Blessed
Virgin. Washington, D.C.-October, 2000
Pat Kalinoski (Regent) with hand on Pam's shoulder

December, 2000
cousin Carol's 60th Birthday Party
L to R Mary Jane, Carol, Pam and daughter, Michelle.

Hammond Family Reunion-June, 1997
Tamworth, New Hampshire

was stationed at Fort Devens waiting to be shipped overseas. Tom just recently retired. He worked in immigrations all his life and traveled all over the world serving his nation.

And a few days before my daughter's wedding, many of us had gathered once more at Chocorua cemetery for a military burial. Uncle Charlie, Tom's father, the last of my mother's generation was buried. All her brothers and sisters have now been laid to rest. And I realized this week before the wedding that my cousins, Marcia, Carol, Mary Jane, Libby, Morris, Tom, Eddie and the New Hampshire cousins are now the "older" Hammond generation. The years are quickly passing by for us and our families.

And I wonder what the Twenty-First Century will bring for our children and their children. Will we retain our faith and become stronger or will it be watered down? Will we be a people of prayer in our nation? Will we honor and defend the many freedoms that we have here in the United States? Will we value life that God has given to us in all its forms? Will we take care of the most vulnerable within our nation: children, the elderly, the handicapped and disabled, the sick and those in need? Will we work honestly and ethically to achieve what we have? Will we give honor and glory to God? Will we value our freedom? Will we value life in all its forms? Only time will tell.

I look at the children and young family members in the Hammond family. I see what hard workers they have become in their daily lives. Many have college educations and almost all own their home. We are not a perfect family by any means but we strive to like one another and enjoy each other's company and come together as family. I guess that's what life is all about: a learning and growing experience as the years pass by.

It was ten o'clock in the evening when I picked up my crutches to leave the wedding reception and I glanced back to the dance floor. It was now very dark but lights circled the dance floor. Michelle could be seen with a guest dancing the night away as her husband, Frank talked with family members.

As I drove away from the reception that evening, June 10, 2000 was a day to cherish as I thought about the many guests that had come, Rose Marino my wonderful neighbor of many years, Mary Jane and her family, my childhood friend Joan Weathers, her husband Dick and daughter,

Kelly. My good friends, Norman and Audrey Hale, sister of my high school friend, Gail Prince who had passed away a few years ago.

I saw Ed and Pat Kalinoski who are very active in their parish at St. John the Evangelist Church. Pat is Regent for the Catholic Daughters of America meetings held at her parish each month. I am also a member of the Catholic Daughters. A trip to the National Shrine of the Immaculate Conception in Washington, D.C. is scheduled soon. Pat and I and many other members will be packing our bags for the trip.

The Catholic Daughters of America stand up for many charitable causes and for many "freedoms" within our nation. Pat said to me before she and Ed left the reception, "Pam, it was the best wedding, Ed and I ever attended." I thanked her for the compliment. Michelle and Frank would be pleased to hear it. And so ended one of the most joyous and memorable events in my life and my daughter's life, her wedding day to her husband Frank Escobedo.

THE PASSING OF CELIA HAMMOND'S GENERATION

I could not help but reflect on how much my mother, Celia, would have loved to have been at my daughter Michelle's wedding to Frank but she had passed away in 1989. I thought of her heart of nurse's compassion for many family members through the years. My mother was always there when a sister or her brother was dying.

When her younger sister, Bertha, was dying of breast cancer in 1974, my mother telephoned, visited and prayed for her. When her brother Eddie "Old Cap" was dying of lung cancer, my mother drove to Tamworth to care for him and to help her sister-in-law, Lottie. When her older sister, Mary, was dying of emphysema, she visited and took care of her for a few weeks until she was admitted into a hospital and passed away in September, 1981. My mother had sold the cottage in Tamworth to her sister many years ago and after Aunt Mary died it was sold once again.

The end of January, 1982, my mother and I attended the funeral of her brother Johnnie. Her brother had been institutionalized for many years after an accident in upper state New York. The funeral was held at Our Lady of Perpetual Help Church in Chocorua. A painting of Our Lady of the Chair can be seen in the front of the church. A lovely statue of St. Therese of Lisieux is located to the left of the altar. After the service my mother and I drove back to Boston in a driving snowstorm. It was treacherous but we arrived home safely.

When my Aunt Catherine was dying of ovarian cancer my mother telephoned and prayed for Catherine, although Catherine became a more private person at the end of her life. I always considered her a second mother to me along with my Aunt Charlotte. I enjoyed the many visits to Conway, New Hampshire to visit Catherine. She had moved to Conway after Uncle Morris had died unexpectedly in 1954. At that time, Uncle Morris, was the caretaker of the Lamb Estate in Milton, Massachusetts. The last time I saw Uncle Morris "Big Daddy" alive was when we had a picnic at Nantasket Beach the week before he died. Uncle Morris, Aunt Catherine and cousin Libby stood on the beach and I snapped their picture, a treasured memory for the future.

At the end of Aunt Catherine's life, her daughter, Libby, arrived from California to care for her mother until she passed away in July of 1986. The last note I received from my Aunt Catherine before she died of cancer was dated March 18, 1986 and she wrote "I was in the Mass General Hospital for nearly a month. My incision across my stomach has healed very well. I am very weak and thin and the doctors and nurses are trying to build me up. I will start having chemotherapy, I hope, soon after the first of April.

Libby has been here for five weeks. Morris came on to Boston for my operation and stayed near-by. He went home last Sunday. Have a nice Easter. Remember me to all the family. A priest and sisters come in with communion for me.

> Love to all,
> Auntie Nin

And at the end of her life, my Aunt Lottie was confined to a nursing home and her daughter, Dorothy, took care of her until her passing. She is another accomplished Hammond woman. Dorothy went back to school and became a lawyer after her children were grown.

L to R: cousin Libby, Aunt Catherine, Uncle Morris
Nantasket Beach Picnic

August 1954

Aunt Lottie-at her home
Tamworth, N.H.
1980's

L to R Michelle, Aunt Charlotte with granddaughter, Chrissy
Thanksgiving Day, November, 1970

Aunt Catherine, Aunt Mary, and Pam
Tamworth, New Hampshire
summer of 1955

Cousin Morris, Pam and Aunt Charlotte
Conway, NH. July, 1986
Aunt Catherine's Memorial Mass

GOD'S BLESSINGS

I could not end this book without talking about the many healings and blessings that our family has received from the hand of God. I thank God for the healing of cancer that I had during 1973 when my daughter was just starting school. Just recently my left arm was healed from over using it at work with the telephone. I could only lift it up a few inches and it hindered almost everything I tried to do, but I persevered and continued on with my work and life in general. It healed quite unexpectedly one Easter Sunday afternoon when I was at cousin Michael's home having dinner with my family. All of a sudden I lifted up my arm and realized that it was healed. Praise God for His blessing, His Easter Blessing for the year 2000.

A couple of years ago I took a pilgrimage to Italy and injured my left knee. I sprained it and when I walked, with my crutches in hand, I felt my knee was going to buckle. One day I visited a very close friend of mine, Marian Manzelli, and over a cup of coffee and a piece of pizza, I told my friend all about the trip. Marian makes the best pizza and it rivals any made in Italy. She's a wonderful cook and baker.

After my visit I returned home and was feeling tired so I rested and fell asleep. And I had a dream. In my dream a priest knelt down and prayed intently over my legs. In the dream I could feel the power and presence of God. When I woke up, seven hours had passed and when I got up and walked, my knee had been healed. Praise God.

Another time, I was experiencing months of aching arthritis throughout my body and went to a healing service. The healing priest, Father Ralph prayed for everyone with arthritis that day. Some people were instantly healed but I recall that I did not experience any healing. Until, that is, I drove home. I parked my car, got my crutches, and started to walk to my door. And then I realized that all the arthritis was gone and that I had experienced the healing love, and the healing touch of Jesus, once again in my life. Praise God.

During the early 1980's, my cousin Carol, with whom I had grown up, was diagnosed with breast cancer. Our family rallied around, her children and other members of the family and many friends also. I helped support her through prayer and by just being there and listening. Carol recovered, but then again in 1984 was diagnosed with breast cancer. She recovered once again and entered nursing school and became a nurse. My cousin Carol now manages a cancer support group and volunteers with the National Cancer Society.

I can recall during this time how a sister-in-law of my cousin Carol named, Doris, became very sick with lymph node cancer. Everyone prayed for Doris. Carol called me one day and said Doris had been admitted into the hospital. The treatments Doris was having were not working.

I was sitting at my desk and wrote Doris a get-well note and enclosed the unfailing prayer to St. Anthony, Saint of Miracles. St. Anthony is such a great saint and I've had a devotion to him for many years. I mailed the note to Doris the next morning and that evening my telephone rang. It was my cousin Carol informing me that Doris was so sick she was not expected to live. Her family was gathered by her bedside. And I remember thinking that I had just sent Doris a get-well card.

A few months later at a family function, Doris walked up to me and said, "Pam, the day your card arrived at the hospital, my husband opened it up and handed it to me. I read the unfailing prayer to St. Anthony, and I now pray it every day." In a couple of weeks Doris was well enough to return home to her family and has now been cancer free since that time.

My cousin, Mary Jane's daughter, Charlotte, at 26 years of age, also became sick with cancer and needed surgery a few years ago. And once again our family members rallied around to support her. Today, Charlotte has been cancer free for many years and has raised two sons, Eddie and Jeffrey.

During December 1998, my cousin Mary Jane was diagnosed with throat cancer. She had been a heavy smoker for many years. Her doctors wanted to remove her larnyx but Mary Jane refused to let them. Instead she opted for a new treatment of cancer at a Boston hospital in which she had a morning and then an afternoon treatment of radiation. Her three children, Susan, Charlotte and Terry rallied around to support her at this time as did the rest of our family.

Before Mary Jane started her treatment, I met her one day for lunch, I remember her smiling and commenting that this lunch might be her last one. I gave my cousin a bottle of blessed St. Anthony oil, the unfailing prayer to St. Anthony, and a Sacred Heart prayer card for healing. I have given the cards out by the hundreds with my hospital work. And, of course, I prayed for my cousin's recovery and well being. Prayer is so very powerful.

Mary Jane responded well to the six weeks of radiation treatment and, hopefully, my cousin will remain cancer free for many more years. And I recall how I had received the bottle of Blessed St. Anthony oil that I had given to my cousin.

One Sunday, after attending Mass at my parish, I decided to drive into Boston to the Italian section of the North End. I drove my hand-controlled car to Boston and found that a festival was taking place in honor of St. Anthony. The festival is held each year and thousands of people attend. I found a parking place, which was a miracle in itself, got my Canadian crutches and started to walk along Hanover Street. I stopped at the corner in front of St. Leonard's Church where two women at a booth were selling bottles of blessed oil. I purchased a bottle and reflected, "Someone will need this." Little did I realize, at the time, that it would be my cousin Mary Jane who also has a devotion to St. Anthony.

My cousin Mary Jane experienced another healing from Jesus a few years ago. She had fallen and broken her arm and it would not heal. So finally her doctors at a Boston hospital wanted to take a piece of another bone and insert it in her arm. I suggested to Mary Jane that we should attend a healing service and pray for God's blessing and healing. We attended a healing service and my cousin's arm was healed. When she returned to the Boston hospital and had X-rays taken, the arm was healed. My cousin Mary Jane said, "Even the nurses knew it was a miracle"!

My cousins and I, when we lived together in Boston with our mothers during the 1940's lived within the borders of St. Anthony's parish in Allston. I believe that St. Anthony has kept an eye on us ever since that time.

Cancer can be a frightening word when one first hears they have the disease. My experience with cancer, has made me a stronger and more compassionate person towards the sick. My heart is always with the sick and those in need. I worked several years in the office at the Cambridge Visiting Nurse Association and enjoyed it. Nurses work so very hard with their many patients. The medical field today can be difficult but very rewarding.

My work now consists of managing a medical escort program for the elderly a few hours a week, for a private agency in my hometown. I love my clients and I find that I am able to help in many ways and to spiritually help the elderly during the weekly contact I have with them. I have a great respect for the caring people who are working in human services especially case managers and social workers. I see how hard everyone works at my agency taking care of the needs of others.

My cousin Susan works with many mentally disabled people in her line of work at a group home in Boston. She often says, "Other people might turn away from the mentally disabled but I love my clients." I believe that it is a calling to work with the disadvantaged, a call from God.

Through the years I have attended many Catholic healing services. My mother, Celia, always loved to attend Father John's healing services at St. Anthony's Shrine in Boston. I have learned so very much from the healing ministry, especially the mercy and love of Jesus for his people. He is so aware and concerned with each one of us personally, our salvation, and with our illnesses and sicknesses. God loves His people, blesses them, and heals them continually. I have seen it happen so many times. I have personally experienced the love and mercy of Christ so many times during my life in such a variety of ways.

No sickness or illness is too complicated or difficult for Christ to heal. It might be a dramatic miracle, or an on going healing or perhaps even the final healing but one thing I do know is that we have a compassionate God who heals.

My brother Peter, at 43 years of age, passed away March 18, 1995 after a long battle with AIDS. He had a drug problem for many years. My mother constantly prayed for her son while she was alive. After she died, I kept my brother in prayer too. Peter had moved out of state for a few years and would telephone me on occasion to say hello.

One day in 1993 my brother John called to tell me that Peter had arrived home and was in a Boston hospital very sick. I went to the hospital and visited him. Peter said to me, "Pam, I came home to die and to make my peace with God. I have AIDS." The next day tests confirmed my brother was dying of AIDS.

Since I did not know anyone personally who was sick with AIDS, I read up on the sickness. I tried to help my brother as best I could and so did the rest of the family. Within a few weeks, Peter was receiving a Social Security check each month and found housing at the YMCA in

Cambridge. AIDS is not an easy illness to deal with, either for the sick person or the family involved.

Each week, Peter would telephone me to tell me how he was doing and managing with his medication. AIDS can be a very lonely disease and a disease of rejection by family and friends. My sister-in-law would invite Peter over for dinner on occasion. My other brothers would meet with Peter and keep in touch until he had to be hospitalized at a public health facility in Boston.

About one month before my brother was permanently hospitalized, Peter telephoned me and mentioned he had visited St. Anthony's Shrine in Boston. He had gone to confession. As an inactive Catholic, it had been many years since he had received the sacrament of reconciliation, forgiveness of sins. I could tell by his voice that Peter felt happy. He received much peace from attending Mass at the shrine each day and then would return home to the YMCA. I recall the day my brother called me to tell me he had gone to confession, I was praying the rosary for him that afternoon. Prayer is powerful. The rosary is a powerful weapon of petition and God and His Blessed Mother listen to petitions.

I recall one day receiving a telephone call from Peter's social worker. My brother was being permanently hospitalized. That evening I visited him at the hospital. I was shocked that Peter did not recognize me and sat motionless in a chair in his room. I had seen my brother a week earlier, and although he was sick Peter was able to hold a conversation. It surprised me that dementia had set in so fast.

As I left the hospital ward that Saturday evening, I passed by the nurse's station and asked what medication my brother was given. The nurse replied he was not on any medication. I recalled that I went home and cried for Peter that evening.

A day later, his social worker called me and I told her of my brother's deteriorating condition. The social worker told me Peter was on some medication and would check with his doctor and get back to me. She telephoned later and told me my brother was on a high dose of mind-altering medication. I went to the hospital immediately and asked the doctor to take Peter off the medication and give another type, if possible. The doctor complied and when I went to visit my brother a few days later, Peter was his old self. He was able to hold a normal conversation for several months until dementia began to set in permanently.

It's important that friends or family members, if possible, keep an eye on the sick, especially the sick that are dying and who are so vulnerable. I do recall the care and concern of the nurses and attendants on the ward where Peter was confined.

Celia (Hammond) McLaughlin
With son, Peter 2 ½
April 30, 1955

L to R, Peter, Celia holding granddaughter, Jenny
and daughter-in-law, Kathy
April, 1980

It was St. Patrick's Day (1995) when I received a telephone call early on Friday morning. Peter had slipped into a coma. My daughter, Michelle, and I went to the hospital and contacted a Catholic church. A priest came and gave Peter the last rites. The next day I visited and Peter was still in a coma. I prayed the rosary for my brother and left for home.

Later that evening I went to the Little Sisters of the Poor chapel and said a prayer for Peter. "God, it's been such a long time for Peter and for the rest of us, his family. Please bring him home." And it had been a long 18 months ordeal for all concerned with my brother's well-being. I distinctly remember the bells in the chapel started ringing. I looked at my watch it was 9 p.m.

I arrived home and a few minutes later the telephone rang. It was my brother's doctor informing me that Peter had just died. I felt a burden had been lifted knowing that he was out of pain and misery and perhaps now in heaven. Two weeks later I received a copy of Peter's death certificate. It noted he died exactly at 9 p.m., the very moment I was in the chapel praying and asking God to bring him home (to heaven), and when the bells began to ring. God listens to prayer and is very concerned with His people who are sick and vulnerable. And I recalled when I saw Peter in the hospital when he first arrived back to Boston. He said, "Pam, I came home to die and to make peace with God." And I do believe that Peter accomplished his goal.

Peter's funeral was held at St. Theresa of Avila Church in West Roxbury where our family home was originally located. The pastor celebrated my brother's funeral Mass with family in attendance. Finally, Peter's remains were brought home to the Hammond Family cemetery in Chocorua, New Hampshire to be buried next to my mother: peace at last.

I have such warm memories of Aunt Charlotte. I recall the many wonderful Thanksgivings and get togethers I had with her, Uncle Don and my cousins through the years. I recall the trips to Lynn Beach, days at Plum Island and trips to their Tamworth home on Hemingway Road. My Aunt always loved red geraniums. Aunt Charlotte, my mother's younger sister, became sick in 1989. My mother kept in close contact with her but Aunt Charlotte passed away in January of that year. At her funeral she looked so peaceful in her red blouse, a rest well deserved. And we all sang her favorite song, "Amazing Grace" at the end of her service. My aunt's passing was another loss for our family and especially for my mother.

On September 14, 1989 my mother, Celia, woke up early one morning with an attack of angina. She was taken by ambulance to a local hospital but died on the operating table a few hours later. A few months earlier, my mother's doctors had suggested an operation. My mother refused and probably due to the fact that 15 years earlier when my mother had open heart surgery, her heart stopped beating on the operating table. But I cannot help but wonder if my mother had the operation, if she might be alive today. Only God knows. My mother was 77 years old at the time of her death which happened on the birthday of her son Peter for whom she always prayed.

My mother had pre-arranged a simple Catholic funeral Mass which was held at her parish church, St. Linus in Natick, Massachusetts. As the flag draped coffin was brought into the church, I could not help but think of her service to our nation during World War II. Many other family members also served our nation well. Robert Hammond is a retired Air Force Major, Roy served in the Navy, my brother, George, served in Viet Nam and is now undergoing treatment for post-tramatic stress due to his tour. Tom Hammond also served in Viet Nam along with John Maller, my cousin Dorothy's husband and Paul Amirault, my cousin Carol's husband. I remember when Paul was given leave, R and R, for a week in Hawaii with Carol, I took care of their two sons, Michael and Paul who now lives in Hollywood, California.

Many family members were also present that day including my mother's three grandchildren, my daughter Michelle and Jenny and Tom. "Nana" took a great delight in them, loved them immensely and enjoyed their company. I had telephoned my daughter at the University of Massachusetts where she was a veterinary science major and a member of the Air Force R.O.T.C. and told her of her grandmother's death. Michelle felt saddened and immediately came home to attend "Nana's" funeral. I watched from my pew as Michelle walked up to the pulpit that day and gave the reading.

I sat in church the day of my mother's funeral, reflecting on her life, the nation she served, her family values, her strong faith and devotion to the Blessed Mother and St. Theresa of Lisieux. I remembered how she always, each and every day, prayed the rosary. I kept my mother's rosary with the gold links and little red hearts and recalled how the rosary links

.

had turned to gold one year when a statue of Our Lady of Fatima came to my home for a nine day visit.

It was Christmas, 1981, and I was attending a healing retreat at the Espousal Center in Waltham, Massachusetts. A woman named Anna turned to me as the retreat was about to end and asked if I would like to have the Lady of Fatima statue in my home for a few days. I agreed and Anna brought Our Lady to my home that year for Christmas.

: I asked some friends to come over one evening and pray the rosary. We prayed the rosary prayers and when my friends were leaving, they asked to leave their rosaries on the folded hands of the statue. The next morning when I got up and walked into my living room, I saw the links of the rosaries had turned gold in color: actually they had turned to brass.

Pam McLaughlin, Lady of Fatima Statue
on which the silver links of the rosary beads turned golden
December, 1981

My mother visited that week and I told her what had happened. She was a bit skeptical at first. She was sitting in a chair praying the rosary when her rosary broke. I told my mother I would send her another one which I did. A few days later, she telephoned to tell me that as she was praying the rosary, the silver links turned to gold right before her eyes. I believe it was a sign to pray the rosary and ask for the Blessed Mother's intercession for all our needs.

I can also recall how Christmas 1981 was so very special for both my daughter, Michelle and myself. She received her Christmas gift in a most unusual way. During October I had asked my fourteen year old daughter what she wanted for a Christmas present. And without any hesitation in her voice she said, "Ma, I want a diamond ring for Christmas!" I was a bit taken back but said, "Michelle, I can't afford a diamond ring but I will get you a birthstone ring instead."

A few days later I returned home from work and parked my hand-controlled car at the elderly handicapped building where I live. I opened the door to get out and immediately saw a tiny sparkling stone on the ground. I picked it up and wondered if it was a diamond. I scotch tapped it to a piece of paper so that I would not lose it. A few weeks later I had to have a piece of jewelry repaired. I took it into Boston to a jeweler named Harold. I also remembered the tiny sparkling stone I had found and brought it along for inspection too.

I told Harold how I had found the sparkling stone on the ground. He laughed and said, "I can't tell you how many people have come into my shop and think they have found a diamond." Harold adjusted his jeweler's eye, held up the stone, examined it and declared, "It's a diamond!" It was a one-third of a carat diamond. I was amazed!

I explained how Michelle had asked me for a diamond ring for Christmas. Harold looked at me and said, "I was just finishing this gold ring. He reached over to his work bench and picked up a lovely ring he had designed with two tiny blue sapphires on the side. In the middle of the ring was an empty space. Harold picked up the tiny diamond with a pair of tweezers and placed it in the empty space. It fit perfectly.

And I recall how on Christmas morning Michelle opened up a blue velvet box and was elated to find a lovely diamond ring. I glanced over and saw the Lady of Fatima statue sitting on a table over looking the festivities on the birthday of her Son, Jesus. It was such a special day;

Christmas Day, 1981. Rosaries had turned golden, a sign to pray the rosary and Michelle had received her Christmas gift; an unexpected diamond ring.

It was my mother's wish that her remains be cremated after the funeral and then taken to New Hampshire for burial. And so it came as no surprise to me that my mother was buried on October first, which happens to be the feast day of St. Theresa of Lisieux to whom my mother had a great devotion. It was not planned as that was the only time available for the attending priest to be present at the gravesite.

As family members gathered together, I recall that Sunday afternoon was one of the most magnificent, Indian summer days New Hampshire had ever seen, warm and balmy with a light wind blowing.

The White Mountain range could be seen in the distance with Chocorua Mountain in full view. My mother had climbed picturesque Mt. Chocorua many times during her lifetime. She went swimming at Chocorua Lake, picnicked on the shores and trout fished from the wooden bridge overlooking the lake with family and friends.

Celia standing on bridge at Mount Chocorua
July, 1966

And now one ordinary woman's earthly life of faith, love, courage and dedication to God and country had come to an end. A nurse for the century, Celia (Hammond) McLaughlin, army nurse and mother remembered.

* * *

Note: On October 18, 1997, the U.S. Post Office issued a first issue stamp for Armed Service Nurses. My mother would have been pleased as October 18th was her birthday and also the feast day of apostle, Saint Luke, who was a doctor during his lifetime. Doctors and nurses work together. Nothing is a co-incidence. It's a God-incident!

EPILOGUE

An interesting incident took place the afternoon after my mother's funeral at St. Linus Church. Our family gathered at the home of my brother Jimmy for refreshments. And when the time was over my brother John asked me if I wanted to go back to my mother's apartment.

John and I drove to the elderly complex on Mill Street and we entered our mother's one bedroom apartment. It was very neat and tidy. A small blue and white silk flower arrangement could be seen on a table. I glanced over to the blue flowered sofa, looked above, and saw Andrew Wyeth's painting of Christina's world. It was a favorite of mine and my mother liked it too.

I noticed that my mother's Bible was open next to her favorite chair. I walked over and glanced down to God's word and read, ·

"They publish the fame of your abundant goodness and joyfully sing of your justice."
Psalm 145:vs.7
The New American Bible

As I read the scripture I could feel the spirit of God speaking to me. And I reflected, "What do you want me to publish, God?" Almost one year after my mother's death, another confirmation was received on August 6, 1990 as I read from my Bible at home.

"Publish his glorious acts throughout the earth.
Tell everyone about the amazing things he does."
Psalms 96:vs.3
The Catholic Living Bible

I could hear the spirit of God speaking to me through His written word but still wondered what God was asking me to publish. It was not clear until all of my mother's World War II victory letters had been collected from my family. And then I began earnestly writing this book, "Celia, Army Nurse and Mother Remembered" during June of 1998.

It was at this time that I began inquiring to our government about receiving my mother's World War II medals. It was difficult because in 1973 a fire destroyed the major portion of records of Army military personnel for the period 1912 through 1959. During the summer of 2001, I contacted my congressman, Michael E. Capuano, and with the help of an aide the medals arrived a few weeks later on August 18th.

I looked at the World War II Victory medal and attached to the red stripped ribbon was a large gold medallion. It depicts a woman on the front and on the back is written "UNITED STATES OF AMERICA 1941-1945, FREEDOM FROM FEAR AND WANT. FREEDOM OF SPEECH AND RELIGION."

And I reflected, "And in our nation, the United States, may we never forget the many freedoms that God has blessed us with and the sacrifices that were made to acquire those treasured freedoms. And may we never be afraid to defend our life values and to protect our nation. Praise God!"

ABOUT THE AUTHOR

Pam McLaughlin, mother and friend to many has been involved in Human Services for a number of years. She has contributed her gifts and talents to the sick, her family and her church.

Afflicted with polio at eleven years of age, Pam has traveled the world since 1964; a model of courage with crutches. As a free lance writer, Pam has reached out with a touch of healing. With the help of her mother's World War II letters, she presents a perspective of family life, faith and courage in spite of life's many obstacles. An amazingly interesting book!

Printed in the United Kingdom
by Lightning Source UK Ltd.
9743500001B